The SPACE

A GUIDE FOR LEADERS

The Space: A Guide for School Leaders

©2020 by Dr. Robert Dillon and Rebecca Louise Hare

All rights are reserved. No part of this publication may be reproduced in any form or by electronic or mechanical means, including information storage and retrieval systems, without permission in writing by the publisher, except by a reviewer who may quote brief passages in review. For information regarding permission, contact Blend Education Publishing. http://blendeducationpublishing.com/.

Published by Blend Education Publishing

Salem, Oregon

http://blendeducationpublishing.com/

Cover Design by Rebecca Louise Hare

Interior Design by Robert Dillon and Rebecca Louise Hare

Editing by Robert Dillon and Rebecca Louise Hare

ISBN: 978-1-7341725-7-7

First Printing: March 2021

WHO IS THIS BOOK FOR?

This is a book with a big tent. It provides inspiration, insights, and ideas for teachers, leaders, and design teams. It is a book to guide PTO partnerships with schools and a text that can empower student design teams and student voice. It is a book for curriculum designers who know the best learning needs amazing spaces. It is a book for superintendents and school boards that are embarking on redesign through budget or bond issue, and it is a blueprint for community partners that want to support schools in ways that leverage change and amplify the impact of schools and communities working together. All designers are welcome here.

A DESIGN PARTNERSHIP

Our projects begin with a deeply human-centered approach that allows us the empathy needed to truly serve and support the teachers and leaders designing spaces around the world. We are deeply grateful for those educators and communities that have invited us into their design work since the publication of our first book in 2016. Many of these projects are featured in the pictures and pages throughout the book, and so many of you have shared your thoughts, ideas, and energy for this book. You have helped us focus on days when the brain was fuzzy, and you provided us with the nudges that we needed to get this project to the finish line.

How do you read this book?

Skip around, start at the beginning... use this book however you need.

WHY LEADERS CONSIDER SPACE PGS. 4-47

← Getting started

IMPACT OF SPACES

HOW SPACE AFFECTS CULTURE

PURPOSEFUL DESIGN

LEARNING SPACE MINDSETS PGS. 48-85

What if you could see your culture come alive in your space?

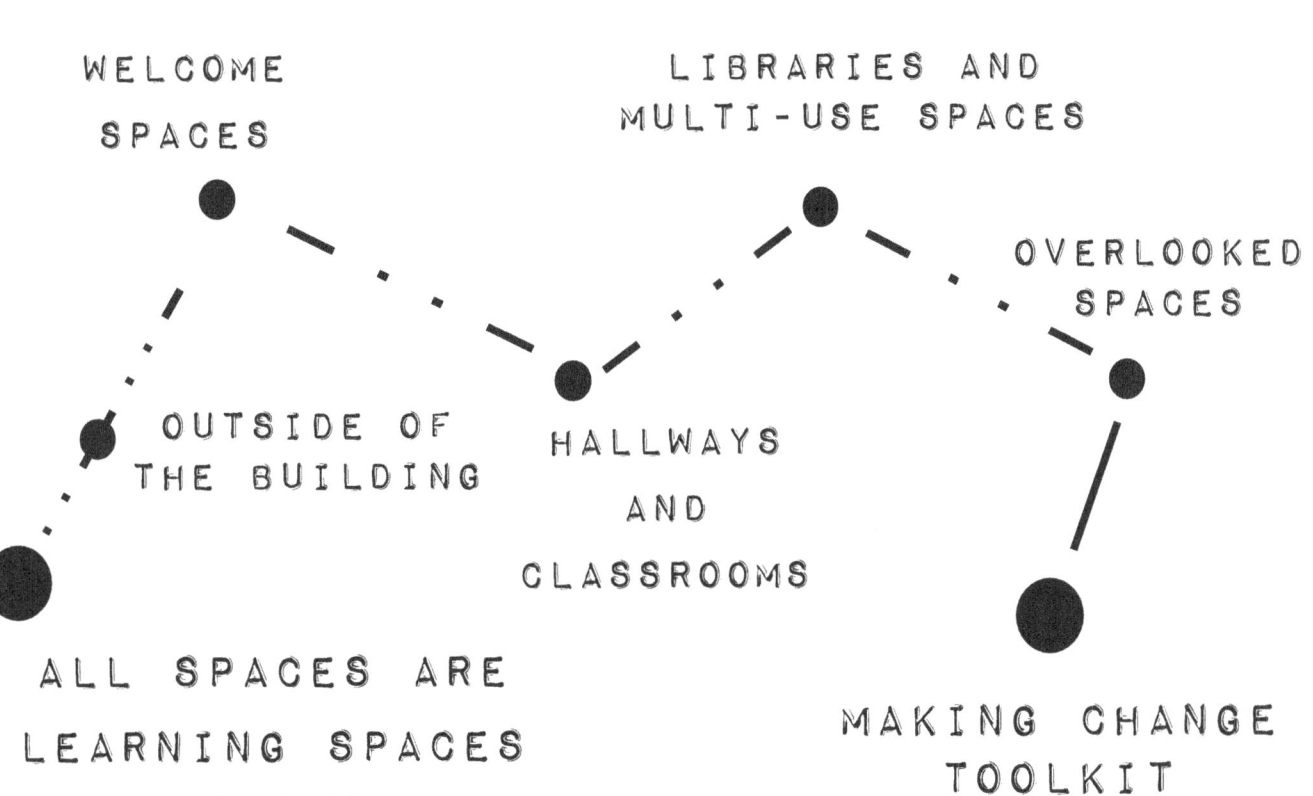

WELCOME SPACES

LIBRARIES AND MULTI-USE SPACES

OVERLOOKED SPACES

OUTSIDE OF THE BUILDING

HALLWAYS AND CLASSROOMS

ALL SPACES ARE LEARNING SPACES
PGS. 86-153

MAKING CHANGE TOOLKIT
PGS. 154-183

WHY LEADERS CONSIDER SPACE: BUILDING CULTURE

"Education does not stand alone, and it cannot be designed as if it did. It exists in a culture."

~ Jerome Bruner

CULTURES EXIST IN SPACES.

NOT A QUICK FIX.

Looking for an antidote?

Learning spaces cannot overcome poor relationships, tired pedagogy, technology as a savior, hungry kids or a disengaged learning community.

It can, however, set the stage for quality learning experiences, support your culture and empower everyone as a leader.

WHY LEADERS CONSIDER SPACE: BUILDING CULTURE

The space says more about
your culture

than any words
you could speak.

Why should leaders care about learning spaces?

Our journey into learning spaces started off more than half a decade ago. Bob was district level Director of Innovation and Rebecca had just transitioned from a designer in an architectural firm to an educator. We had a tiny budget and a big idea: learning spaces don't have to be expensive and out of reach.

It started off with just a handful of spaces in one small mid-western district with a budget that was equal to a few teacher laptops. Then, as we supported more teachers, librarians and school counselors to change their spaces, we were asked to write a blog post to help other teachers. That post turned into a book (*The Space: A Guide for Educators*) that we hoped would help any teacher, on any budget start to feel empowered as a learning space designer.

In the years since, we have continued working with districts to transform learning through spaces and have come to understand that to do this work well we cannot rely on rogue teachers hacking their spaces in isolation without support. We need systemic, building-wide initiatives, common language and goals. We need leaders to see the connections between academic achievement, social emotional learning, the infusion of technology and the space in which those things happen. We need leaders who understand the connection between culture and space.

WHY LEADERS CONSIDER SPACE: BUILDING CULTURE

THINK ABOUT THIS...

As a leader, ask yourself, does your building hold people back or elevate people?

SPACE IS GOING TO UNITE US

What type of culture do you want?

Culture of Compliance

Teachers do what is expected of them, but are rarely truly invested in the outcome (school culture). They may feel that they are competing with other teachers to gain approval and resources from leaders.

What does this mean? All of the energy and momentum is supplied by the leader.

Culture of Commitment

Teachers have agency and input into both the culture and the vision of the school. Since they are involved, they become more invested in the outcomes. Other teachers are seen as collaborators, not competitors.

This creates more buy-in that enables leaders to become facilitators and supporters of a common vision.

ALLOW YOUR SPACES TO UNITE EVERYONE UNDER A SHARED VISION OF EXCELLENCE.

Expanding a Culture of Commitment

Dr. Adam Pease, Assistant Superintendent at Chappaqua Central School District

Project: Re-design of a high school learning wing.

Why did you focus on reshaping the learning culture for your project?

Doing so led to an increased clarity of our vision for active, project-based learning in spaces that support collaboration, technology integration, and authentic learning experiences for all students.

Where did you find success?

The single most powerful result of improving instructional spaces for us has been the professional learning that these new spaces have inspired. Conversations about the intentional design of instructional space quickly transition to lively discussions about improving classroom climate, progressive instructional methods, the development of modern curriculum, and authentic assessment practices.

What other learning came from the project?

We are just beginning to understand the extent to which changes in instructional space actually drive improvements in curriculum, pedagogy, and assessment practices.

What advice would you give others working on similar things?

The purposeful design of instructional space is not only a way to positively impact student learning but also a powerful gateway which leads to new and exciting professional learning paths for educators to explore.

Responsive Spaces and Culture

Dr. Jana Parker, Director of Innovation and Gifted Education at Lindbergh School

Project: Re-design of an elementary counselor's space.

Why did you focus on social emotional learning for your project?

School counseling in the traditional sense was in need of a paradigm shift. Many of our students came to us with trauma and needed a space that was not only warm and inviting, also fluid and flexible that could meet the multiple needs of our students. The intent was to alter the image of what had always been seen as a counseling "office," the impact was far greater than we could have imagined.

Where did you find success?

We saw a dramatic decrease in office referrals because students had an opportunity to get their sensory needs met. Even students without sensory needs were provided with tools and opportunities to de-escalate, before making a negative choice. Teachers also saw a transfer of the strategies and lessons taught in the new responsive space.

What other learning came from the project?

Many of our staff wanted a similar feel and design for their own classrooms. The decorated classrooms, often seen on social media, were quickly replaced with simple, student-centered, neutral design schemas that allowed for maximum movement. Various spaces were created with great intention and student input providing for more student ownership.

What advice would you give others working on similar things?

While there was risk-taking involved, having the "why" and fortitude to do what is best for students was always at the forefront. I did not readily accept no and found ways to work around most obstacles. A little personal elbow grease also went a long way.

WHY LEADERS CONSIDER SPACE: BUILDING CULTURE

Momentum for Change:

Where is your culture headed? How will your spaces support this vision?

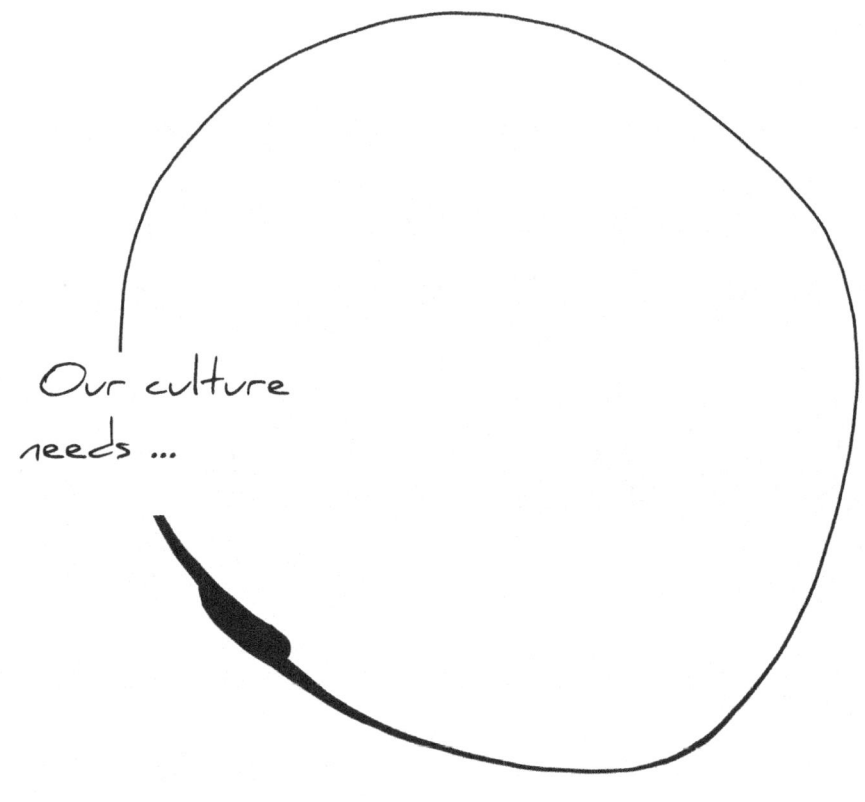

USE THIS PAGE TO RECOGNIZE HOW YOUR SPACE IMPACTS YOUR CULTURE.

it looks like...

it feels like...

it results in...

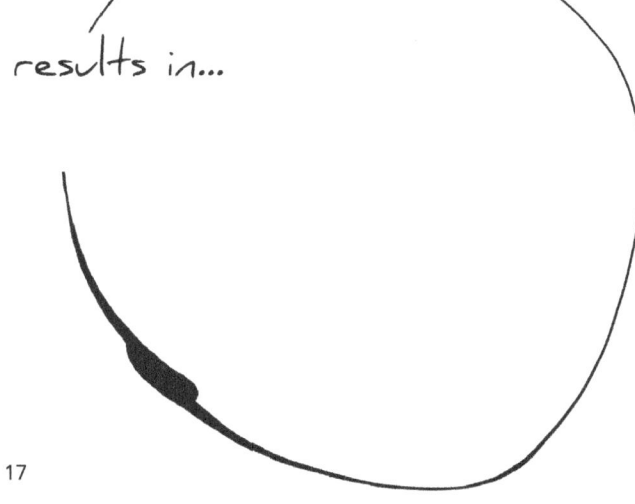

WHY LEADERS CONSIDER SPACE: PURPOSE

THE RESEARCH IS CLEAR THAT

when we **increase choice and agency** *it then* **results in greater engagement and joy in students.**

And research also shows that

engagement and joy are the leading indicators for kids to achieve and grow.

(check out Gronneberg, Johnston, 2015)

So don't let the conversation about space begin with someone asking about whether it will raise test scores.

WHY LEADERS CONSIDER SPACE: PURPOSE

WHY INTEGRATED DESIGN MATTERS

The journey to creating your spaces is just as important as the destination. A literature review from Great Britain explains ...

"The second striking finding from this review is that it is the extent to which, and the ways in which, school users are engaged in the school design process that determines the success or failure of the resulting design. The message is clear. School designs cannot be imposed nor bought off–the–shelf. **Success lies in users being able to articulate a distinctive vision for their school and then working with designers and architects to create integrated solutions.**

The open-plan classroom movement showed that purely physical design solutions that are not owned by their users or supported with effective systems and behaviour change will not work."

The Impact of School Environments: A Literature Review: The Centre for Learning and Teaching-School Education, University of Newcastle

WHY LEADERS CONSIDER SPACE: PURPOSE

HOW WILL YOU LEAD THIS WORK?

No space is neutral. Everyday, every space affects us. It can prime us to feel creative, valued, safe, and ready to learn. We no longer have the luxury to wait before we act on learning space design. What will be your first steps as a leader? Will you respond to the needs of your spaces, or will you anticipate them?

RESPONDING TO SPACE NEEDS

wait for stuff to break and then fix it

LET THE FACILITIES TEAM DEAL WITH IT

limit conversations and empowerment

CONSIDER ONLY IF THERE IS FUNDING

INVITE CONVERSATIONS

develop a designer's mindset

CREATE A TEAM

ANTICIPATING SPACE NEEDS

find and raise funding

CHOOSE A FOCUS

visit some amazing school spaces

Steps for Success

Every leader needs the support of systems and structures to bring their ideas to life. This section provides some practical ways to begin the work to leverage the power of learning spaces throughout the building.

Start with your own clarity of purpose. Sharing your purpose with your school allows everyone to know that they are supporting thoughtful ideas and not just the latest trend. In this section, we introduce the hierarchy of purpose as a mental model that can support your focus, goals and the direction of your design team. We give you ideas about how to form your educator and student design teams and how to begin this journey.

Thinking is good. Actions are better.
Let's get to work.

WHY LEADERS CONSIDER SPACE: PURPOSE

CHOOSE YOUR FOCUS

Your team can approach learning space design in a lot of ways. Many schools start with comfort and choice. Those can have positive effects on the emotional needs of students and increase their agency, but spaces can have an impact in so many other ways. We can design spaces that facilitate the types of learning experiences we want and support systemic changes like inquiry-based learning and trauma-informed classrooms. Let's start from the top:

Systemic Change

What are your big initiatives? Equity? Re-thinking assessment? Student outcomes? Whatever your focus, learning spaces should not be left out of the equation. They can be a driving force and a physical manifestation of your vision.

Learning

Are there new teaching methods you want to employ and support? Spaces should be designed to support the learning experiences within them. When space and instruction are aligned, there is a multiplier effect.

Choice

We cannot get better at making decisions unless we have choices to make. Providing students with a choice in where, how and when they do their work helps increase their autonomy and agency. This doesn't mean that students get to make all of the decisions, but choice is an empowering feature of each classroom.

Comfort

Is the space designed to comfortably support those working and learning? Stress continues to hamper excellent learning. Intentional design can help students feel less stress when they enter the classroom.

FORM A DESIGN TEAM:

Now is the time to expand the voices and ideas around your focus. Use these design team roles so that everyone has a purpose on your team. Check the next few pages on creating a student design team as well.

Instruction Focused Designer

Keeps the focus on effective instructional practices and how the spaces can enhance and support them.

Social/Emotional Focused Designer

Keeps the focus on effective methods for social-emotional learning and how the space can support it.

Designing in isolation removes the possibility of the best ideas coming from the wisdom of the room.

WHY LEADERS CONSIDER SPACE: PURPOSE

Equity and Agency Focused Designer

Keeps the focus on how the space can support culturally responsive learning and student agency.

Strategic Goals Focused Designer

Keeps the focus on how the space can support district, building and discipline strategic goals.

Principal Designer/ Work Place Wellness Focus

Has the authority and agency to oversee the process, and is good at building and maintaining commitment to the goals. They are supportive and not controlling of other designers. They keep the focus on the wellness of faculty and staff, including ADA compliance.

Form a Student Design Team

Along with your faculty and leader team, create a design team comprised of students. Even ten students can give your school great insight, empathy and the students' ownership of the space and process.

Let their work be active

Students support the design process most effectively when they are:

Brainstorming

Get their ideas, both verbal and visual.

Giving Feedback

What do they think of the plan?

Setting Up The Space

Invite them to build the first iteration.

Re-configuring The Space

Ask, "How can we make it better?"

Student Design Team

Include a cross-grade level team, give them the title of co-designers and meet with them regularly.

Community

The community is important, but beware that they do not hijack the spaces or the process. This should be driven primarily by those who use the spaces.

WHY LEADERS CONSIDER SPACE: BUILDING CAPACITY

Teacher-Leader Design Team

Gather Student Input

This can be done as a Q&A, a survey, a set of sticky notes or informal conversations. Whichever works best, just don't leave these groups out of the conversation at any stage. If this is asynchronous, you can spend this meeting looking at the responses.

Student Questions:

- *What spaces in the building are your favorite places to learn?*
- *What spaces in the building seem old and tired?*
- *What are three spaces that you think need to be redesigned?*

Gather Community Input

This is a great opportunity to gather information from parents, alumni, and long-time community members as they have unique perspectives about the school spaces.

Community Questions:

- *What spaces feel like the heart and soul of the building?*
- *What elements are central to the identity of the school building?*
- *What changes could positively impact teaching and learning?*

HIERARCHY OF PURPOSE

How can your learning space work enhance your current initiatives? →

Systemic Change

Learning
Syncing instructional practices with space design.

Establish a strong foundation. ↙

Choice
Providing students options about where and how they learn.

Comfort
Creating a psychologically safe environment, supporting a variety of postures, lowering environmental stresses.

SET SOME GOALS:

We want our spaces to support our strategic initiatives including:

_____

_____

_____

We want our spaces to support our learning methods including:

_____

_____

_____

We want our students to have choices of how and where to work and learn. They might include:

_____

_____

_____

We recognize the need for ergonomic design for our learners and their comfort. We know the look and feel of spaces are important to students' well being.

We strive to...

_____

_____

_____

HAND TOOLS

Iterate

Design

CHARLES C. JAMES
Guide to Imagination and Design Thinking
D!LAB

imagination
inspiration
innovation

WHY LEADERS CONSIDER SPACE: BUILDING CAPACITY

Now you are ready!

BEGIN THE DESIGN TEAM JOURNEY

You have determined who is going to support this work, so it is now time to get started. We have mapped out four essential phases for your design team to build consensus and commitment to this work. This doesn't have to be a semester's worth of meetings, it can happen quickly. The more time you spend building capacity with your team, the longer learning space designs will remain a priority after your tenure as the leader of the building.

The Phases:
- The Launch
- Building Awareness
- Space Priorities
- Action Planning

* Plus, We Added A Leader's Survival Guide

Each phase should be engaging and fun.
Try to have your gatherings in neutral and inspiring spaces.

PHASE ONE: THE LAUNCH

Positive energy is essential for this work. This includes making your meetings a psychologically safe space where all are welcome and varied voices and ideas can emerge.

Don't forget to include your student designers!

1. Assign Roles for the Process

You can do this two ways: allow each team member to self-select based on their interests and skills or you can invite them to a specific role. *See page 26 for the different roles you will need.*

2. Develop Goals and Outcomes

Create a list of the desired outcomes for the spaces you are designing. Once you have this list, have the design team prioritize it. This activity uncovers a deeper understanding of individual thinking about the work.

This is your opportunity to determine, "When this work is finished, we'll know we have been successful because...." (*Write this sentence stem on a large surface and let individuals respond independently, then work as a team to bring the language and ideas to a consensus.*)

3. Learn the Space Mindsets

These mindsets create a common way of thinking about space and begin to leverage change before any purchasing ever occurs. Building these mindsets among teachers and leaders has allowed deep change to happen in many schools and districts. The mindsets are discussed in detail beginning on page 48.

Spending time here will make your changes sustainable.

4. Establish a Common Language

Take a moment to make sure your design team has a common language around terms: learning spaces, flexible, agile, design, active learning ... just to name a few.

(Try writing each word on the board and have your team share what they think it means. Work to have everyone agree on one general definition for each term. Doing this will help curb confusion later in the process. Each time a new word comes up, do not assume that everyone agrees on what it means. Take a minute and define it as a group.)

5. Plan The Next Steps

Leaving this phase with clear next steps will provide the design team with momentum and set you up for success as a team.

PHASE TWO: BUILDING AWARENESS

It is easy to become desensitized to environments where we spend a lot of time. These five areas will help the team have a deeper awareness of what is working in our spaces and what needs to change.

1. Build your Awareness Skills

Take your team outside with the objective of noticing the space in a fresh way and heightening awareness. To do this, have everyone make an inventory of what they see (door, sign, bush, etc.). Additionally, have everyone share how the outside of the building makes them feel. New understandings will emerge from this time of deep observation.

This is a great strategy to invite others like parents, community members and other building leaders to do with you as well.

2. Whole School Walk

Move inside and continue to have your team practice at observing. Each person should find five to seven spaces or details they had never noticed.

This activity is designed to disrupt our typical behaviors and routines in the space. Go through the whole school, explore even the parts of the building that are rarely used. Use this time to help everyone build awareness so that later, you can find opportunities for change.

3. Look Critically

Next, start to identify small spaces in the building that don't align with the mission and vision. It can be as small as a sign, or the placement of a trash can. Ask the team members to explain why they think it does not align. The rest of the team listens without judgment.

Every space sends out non-verbal messages about the school. They shape the energy and attitude of the building and affect each of us differently. Spaces can also unintentionally inhibit equity efforts by sending a message of low expectations and making people feel unwelcome or unsafe.

4. Find Easy Wins

Then, find some easy things that can be fixed immediately. Remove an old poster. Fix a broken ceiling tile. Tidy up.

You don't need to wait to finalize a grand plan. These actions empower the team and showcase that small changes can have big impact. It also builds momentum and positive energy around the work.

5. Give The Next Steps

Finally, prepare the team for taking action. Give them a quick preview of the next two phases.

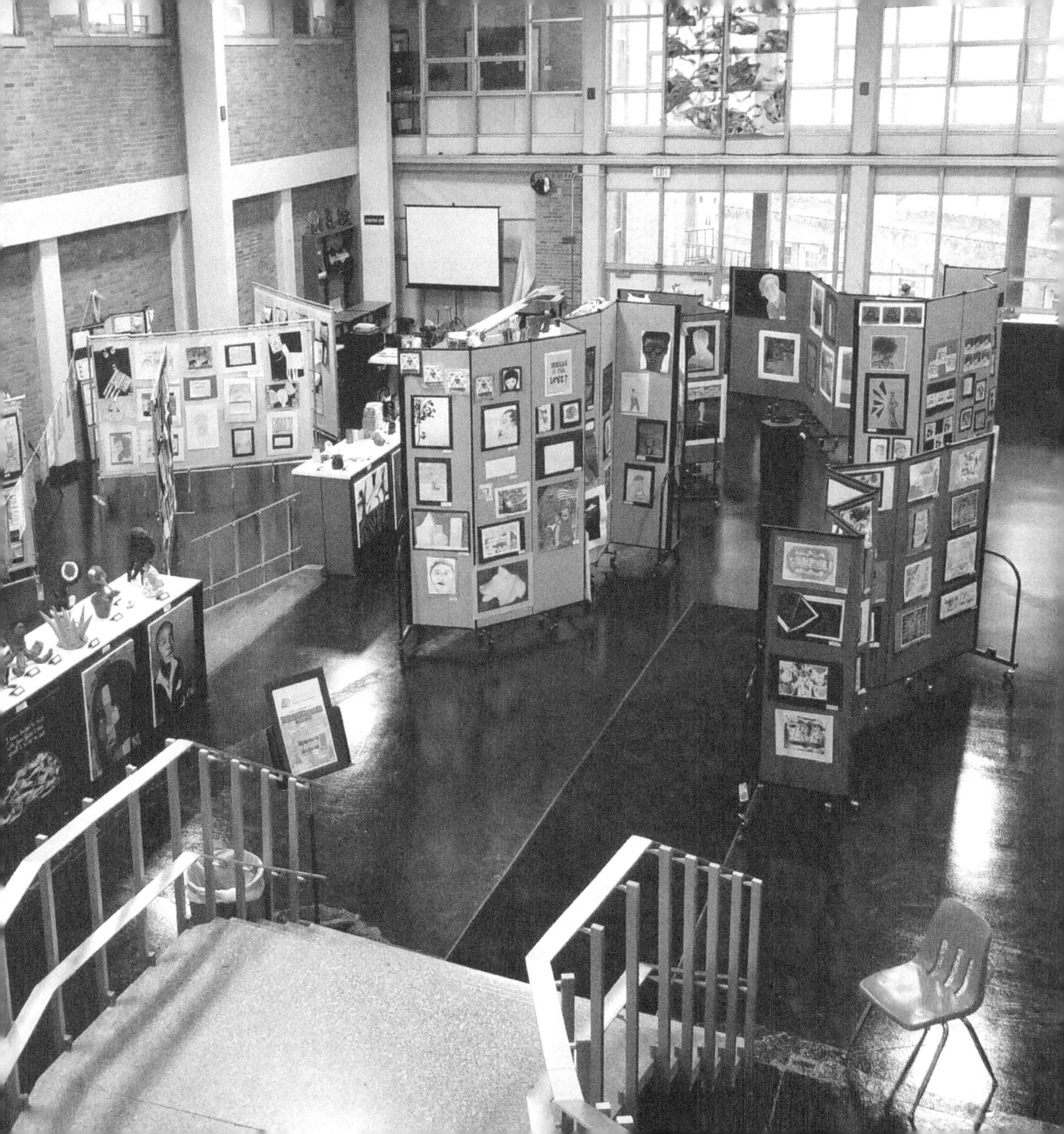

GREEN SPACES

TEACHERS' LOUNGE   FRONT ENTRANCE

HALLWAYS   PARKING

DROP OFF AREA   SIGNAGE

DO A SCHOOL WALK-THROUGH: WHAT DO THESE ELEMENTS CURRENTLY SAY ABOUT YOUR GOALS?

OFFICES   AFTER-CARE

LIBRARIES   IEP MEETING AREAS

RESTROOMS

CAFETERIA   CLASSROOMS

BULLETIN BOARDS

How do these spaces make you feel about your school?
Proud? Frustrated? Embarrassed?

PHASE THREE: SPACE PRIORITIES

Priorities Protocol

Use this protocol to sort your priorities. Using this structure allows for an orderly way for all ideas to be represented prior to action planning.

- **BRAINSTORM ALL NEEDS - 10 MINUTES**

    Get all ideas on the table based on the whole school walk and other observations.

- **GENERATE NEED CLUSTERS - 5 MINUTES**

    Bring ideas into design clusters. This could include: lighting, paint, and/or accessibility.

- **PRIORITIZE WITHIN CLUSTERS - 5 MINUTES**

    Rank each of the projects in the clusters. This begins to bring the top priorities to the surface.

- **DISCUSS POTENTIAL IMPACT - 15 MINUTES**

    Refer back to the Hierarchy of Purpose (page 30). Lots of change can look good, but lack impact on learning, culture and strategic goals.

- **CHOOSE FIRST FIVE ACTIONS - 10 MINUTES**

    Decide on where to begin based on the actions that can lead to impactful wins.

- **DESIGN MESSAGING - 5 MINUTES**

    Each design team member should be able to articulate why these are the priorities and how they support the school. Don't leave it to chance.

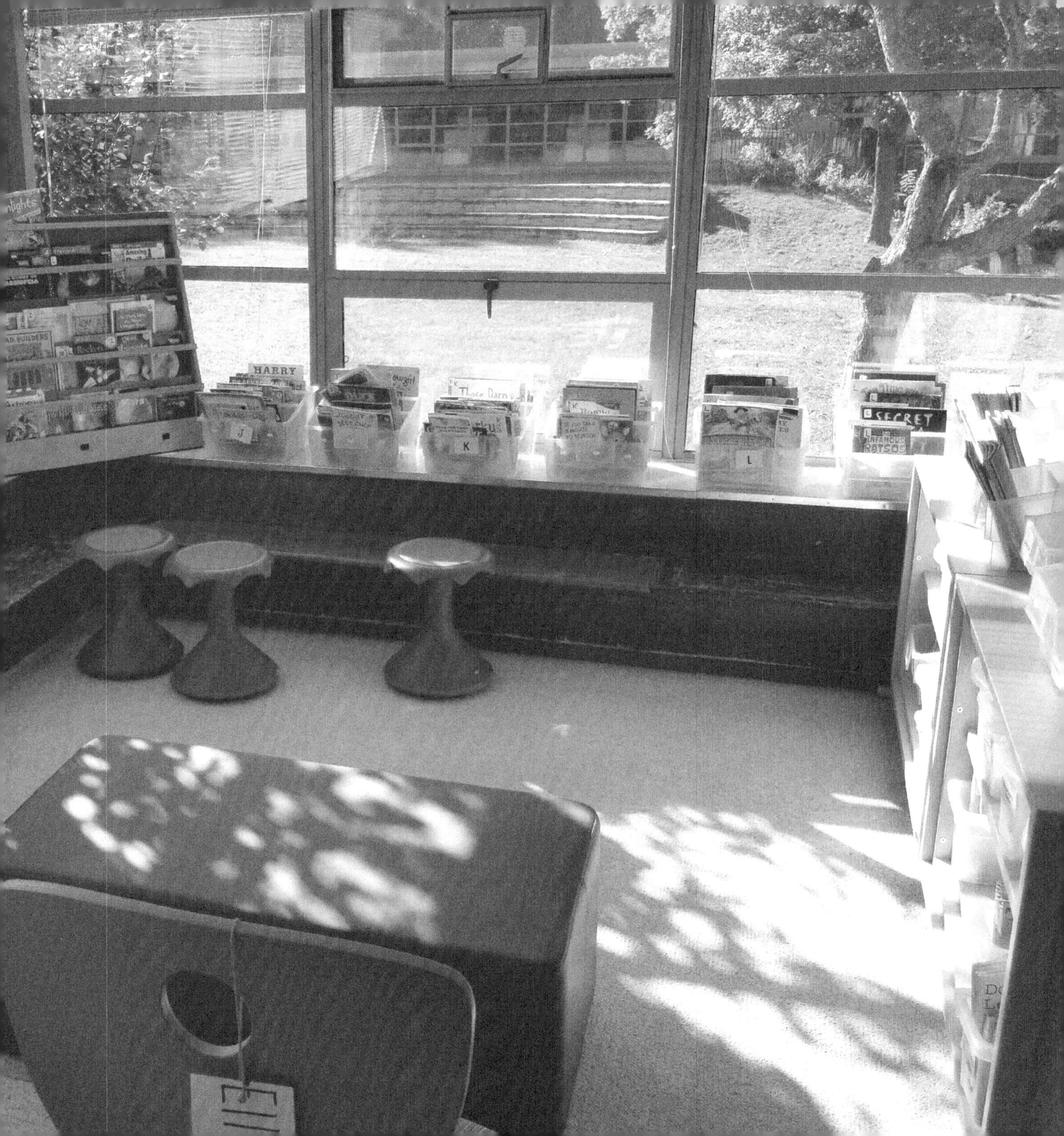
HARRY
Those Darn
J
K
L
SECRET
INFAMOUS RATSOS

PHASE FOUR: ACTION PLANNING

It is time to take your priorities and begin to design action plans that can bring your changes to life.

What changes can you make in the next five days? (Think easy wins):
_____
_____
_____

What changes can you make in the next five weeks? (Think impactful changes):
_____
_____
_____

What changes can you make in the next five months? (Think larger scale work):
_____
_____
_____

(Repeat the steps above as long as you have learning spaces.)

INVITE CONVERSATIONS

hack a space together and test it out

EMPTY A ROOM

ORDER SAMPLE FURNITURE

find and raise funding

CHOOSE ONE FOCUS

visit some amazing school spaces

Are you wanting more details on where to start? We wish that we could script the path, but space design is a custom experience, not a standardized playbook. There are lots of potential answers on the pages ahead, but as you begin consider these pieces...

DESIGN TEAM SURVIVAL GUIDE

The best planning can fall short without insights on how to execute the plan. Use the suggestions in this survival guide to avoid the common pitfalls of leading new design projects.

Tips for Choosing Furniture

- ASK FOR SAMPLES / BUY ONE

    Be the leader who empowers teachers and students to test furniture before you commit to buying in volume. Vendors can provide items that can be tested in your space before purchase.

- BALANCE VALUE AND DURABILITY

    There is a fine balance between how much something costs and how long it will last. Not every purchase needs to last for decades and not every item should be the cheapest available. Remain intentional in both areas as you make final purchases.

- COORDINATE FINISHES

    Furniture tends to move around buildings and even between them. Choose items that will work together no matter where they go. Pick a color theme use the same wood tones so that when your spaces evolve, they can remain coherent.

- UNDERSTAND LEAD TIME

    Before you commit to a vendor or certain pieces, check the lead times. They can easily run twelve weeks. So plan ahead and be ready to make decisions by a set date.

Tips for Installation

- **EMPOWER MAINTENANCE/OPERATIONS**

    These professionals will be key to the success of a project; be clear with expectations and responsibilities. Know the guidelines on who can install, assemble and repair.

- **STORAGE, BUILD, INSTALL**

    Most schools are not equipped to receive a warehouse of furniture nor have space to build and install it. Have a clear plan.

- **CHECK THE CODES**

    The Fire Marshall, union representatives and ADA compliance guidelines can help guide you. No one wants to do double work.

- **SET-UP PARTY**

    Include the designers (teachers and students) in the initial setting up of the space. See how it feels, make it a celebration and let it evolve from the plans. Don't let those outside of the design team dictate arrangement.

- **FINAL TOUCHES**

    Once you place the main elements, plan on purchasing a few final things like window treatments, accent lighting, pillows and decor. These final touches can really tie it all together and make the desired impact.

Keeping the Design Spirit Alive

Celebrate the end of the initial phases of the work. Lots of hard work has gone into rethinking the space for teaching and learning. Now get back into design mode by:

- **Collecting Data:** Gather reactions of students and teachers as well as observational data about behavior and learning.
- **Keep Evolving:** Model movement agile furniture to new configurations. Classrooms and other spaces can get quickly locked into one layout despite the flexible furniture choices.
- **Release Control:** One person can't be the design champion. Empower others to bring forward new ideas and let other leaders emerge.

Also we suggest

The Goldilocks Principle (page 121) to create the "Just Right Language" for your furniture choices

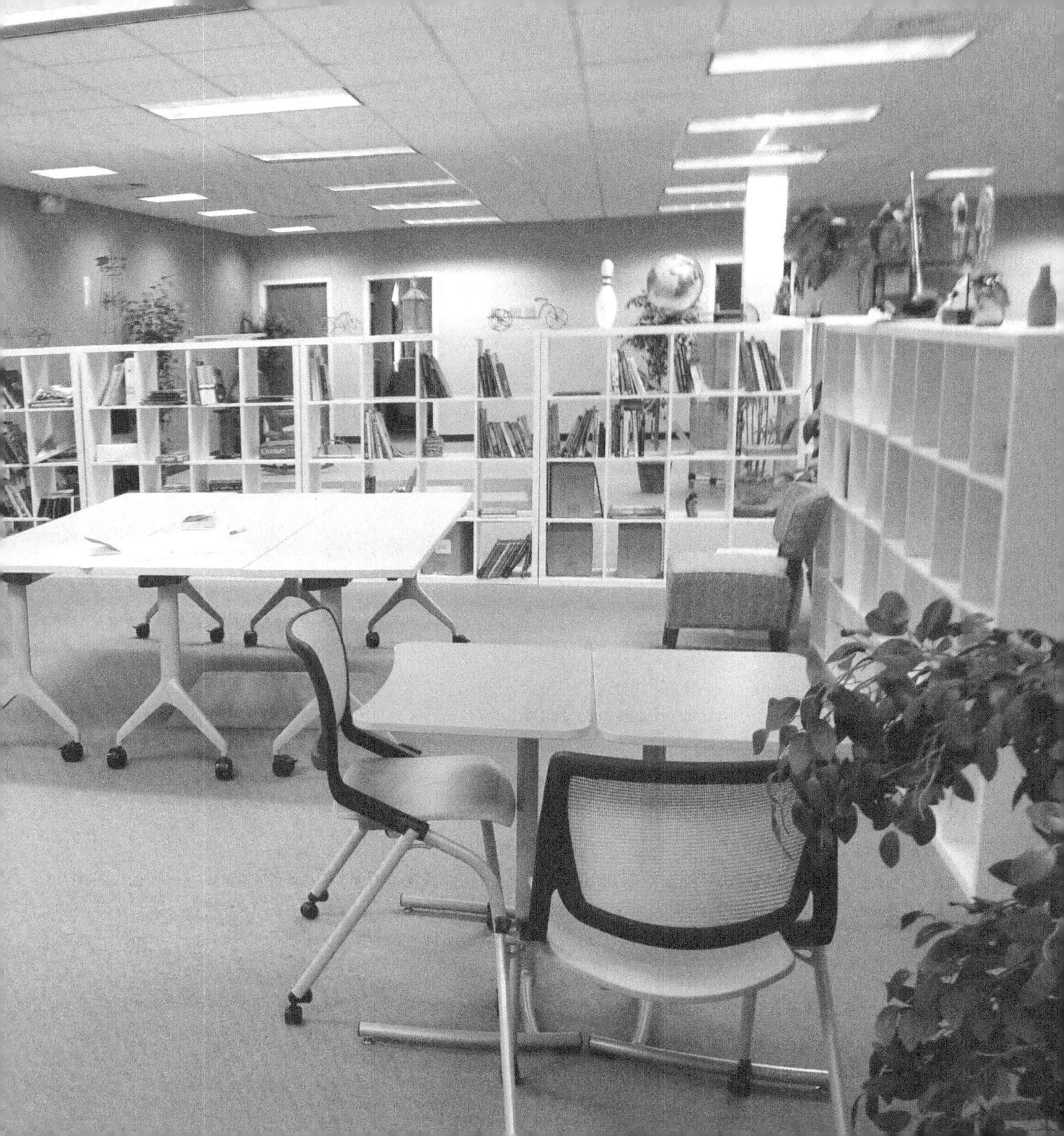

~~Hopefully~~ *Because of our work*, we will have made these improvements by the end of next school year... _____

_____

so years from now, our spaces will impact learning and culture by...

_____

_____

_____

Don't forget these plans as well

1. Communication Plan
2. Budget Plan
3. Measurement Plan

See Toolkit in Back For Details

Mindsets for Intentional Design

Skip around, start at the beginning... use this book however you need.

WHY LEADERS CONSIDER SPACE PGS. 4-47

IMPACT OF SPACES

HOW SPACE AFFECTS CULTURE

PURPOSEFUL DESIGN

You are Here →

LEARNING SPACE MINDSETS PGS. 48-85

"Once your mindset changes, everything on the outside will change along with it."

Steve Maraboli

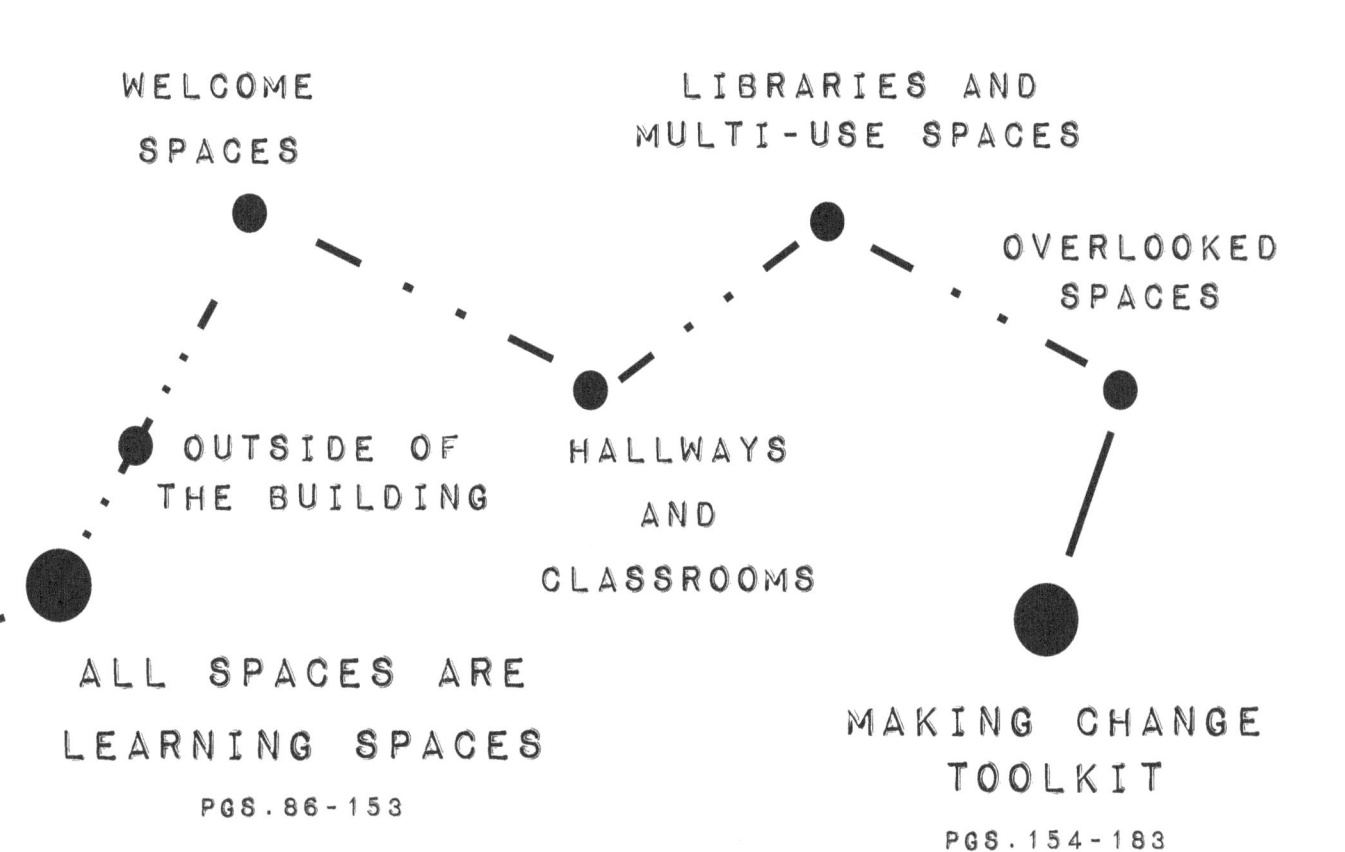

WELCOME SPACES

LIBRARIES AND MULTI-USE SPACES

OVERLOOKED SPACES

OUTSIDE OF THE BUILDING

HALLWAYS AND CLASSROOMS

ALL SPACES ARE LEARNING SPACES

PGS. 86-153

MAKING CHANGE TOOLKIT

PGS. 154-183

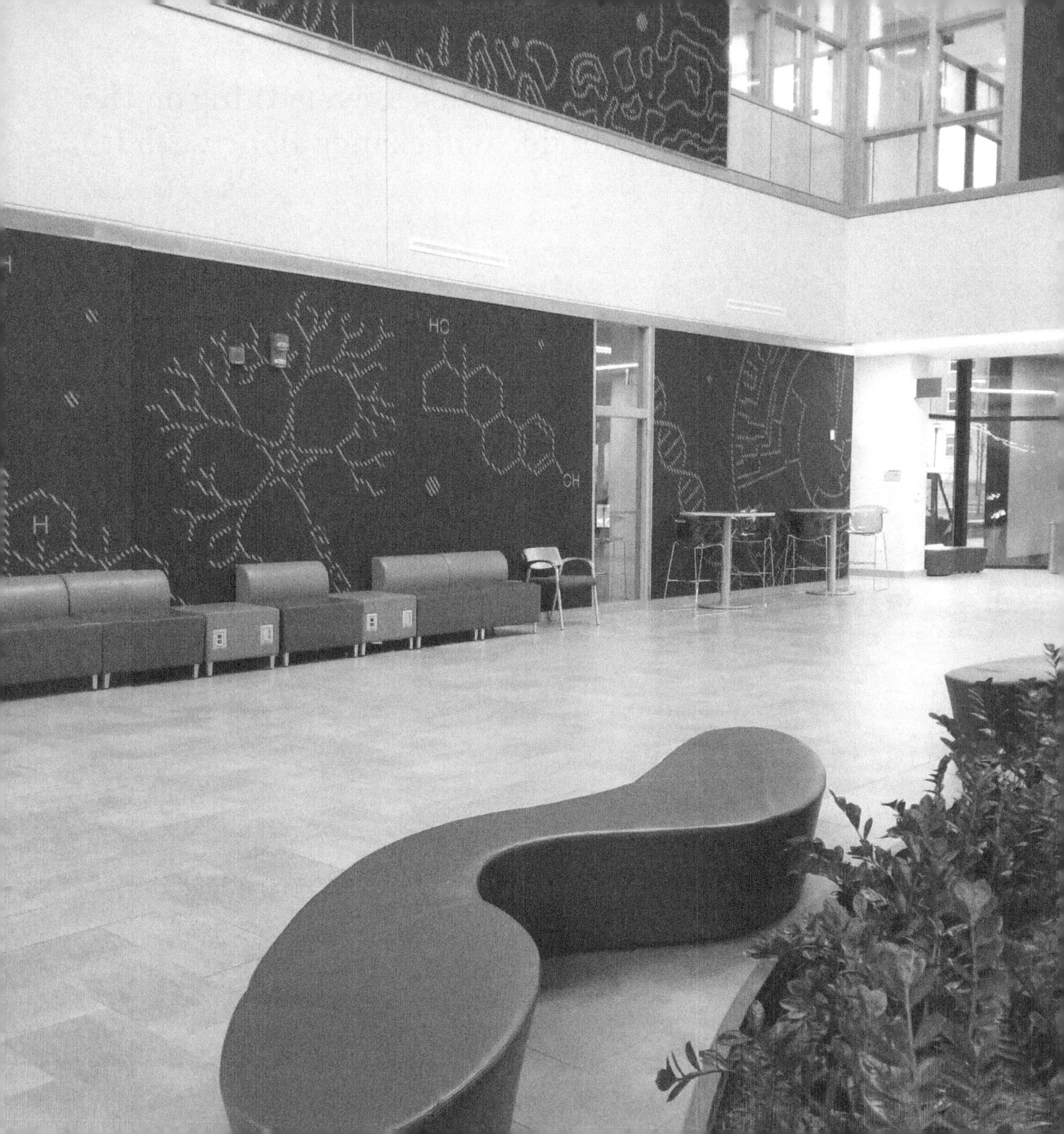
HO
OH
H

MINDSETS

COMMON LANGUAGE & GOALS

It doesn't matter if you have one million dollars, or none. Try starting the journey with your design team and then the entire staff by sharing language and goals through the introduction of "design mindsets" that get to the *how* we transform learning through spaces. This work allows members your school to reflect, in their own time, on how these concepts affect the learning in their spaces. Having these mindsets in the school DNA goes a long way to building a culture of commitment.

We have a few that we have seen empower whole schools:
- Equity and Agency
- Addition by Subtraction
- Push vs. Pull
- Process over Product

These mindsets are not just for physical spaces

They can help us plan out virtual learning too!
See pages 168-175 to learn how the mindsets can apply to distance and virtual learning.

Why Design Mindsets?

Lindsey Blass, San Francisco Unified School District

Rebecca has been consulting with SFUSD and developed the design mindsets with Lindsey for the Tech-Enabled Personalized Learning Pilot and many other learning space initiaves. The mindsets support both technology integration and learning space design.

Why did you focus on the mindsets?

Our district engaged a team of teachers from across San Francisco for a technology-enabled personalized learning pilot to explore models for powerful integration of technology. We recognized that we couldn't ignore the physical environment with the instructional shifts we were advocating for, which included increased opportunities for students to collaborate and create. We wanted to empower teachers to design environments where students had agency, choice, and voice in their learning experience and to keep students who had been historically underserved at the forefront of this design. With this, we recognized that in order for practice and physical environments to shift agency to students, we would need intentional work around our mindsets that created the conditions for a transformed teaching and learning experience.

What new learning came from the project?

Our pilot teachers and administrators felt empowered to serve their students in distance learning as well. They saw how the skills were transferable with the right foundation in place. Distance learning requires students to take agency and ownership of their learning. Throughout our pilot, teachers had already laid a foundation where students were given choice in their learning process and product, as well as a voice to say where and how they do their best learning. This seamlessly supported the level of agency students needed to have for themselves in a distance learning environment.

What advice would you give others working on similar things?

It's not about the stuff: *For districts embarking on this work, don't start with "the stuff". Our teachers and administrators engaged in nearly five months of professional learning and lesson design cycles before gaining access to flexible furniture, and in reflection teachers identified this as a key factor in their success.*

Partner in this work: *Teachers who participated with grade-level colleagues found they had the ongoing support needed to truly engage in iterative design in service of all students.*

Advocate for the work to be supported: *If you are a teacher, be transparent with your administrator and colleagues on the work you are doing with the design mindsets so they can become your supporters. Teachers can offer to share a success (and a struggle) at a staff meeting and bring their colleagues along for the journey. Administrators can broadcast successes of their teachers and the work, and in turn be the lead change agent and advocate for their teachers.*

WHERE DID YOU FIND SUCCESS?

The design mindsets provided us with a common language around our work, and allowed teachers to express areas of success or struggle in the instructional shifts they explored. In our research partnership with Stanford University, we found success both in terms of how teachers leveraged technology, as well as the physical environment:

TECHNOLOGY

Teachers described:

- *Greater confidence in their ability to integrate technology.*
- *Shifts in thinking about the purposes technology can serve and which uses are most meaningful, all of which impacted their practice in concrete ways.*
- *Increased comfort and skill with tech among students and in some cases students helping lead or support activities.*

FLEXIBLE ENVIRONMENTS

Teachers reported that:

- *They implemented more flexible classroom routines.*
- *Students showed more ownership and responsibility overall for their actions in the classroom.*
- *Students engaged in more collaboration and interaction.*
- *In some cases, students whose behavior had been problematic before showed much better participation and engagement.*
- *Flexible routines allowed teachers to reflect more on what is permissible in the classroom and be more inclusive of students with different preferences.*

Why it matters:
Addition by Subtraction

When we have a perceived need, we look for something to acquire in order to meet that need. However, if we start by removing elements that build up over time, we begin to free up space to be used more effectively. Everything we bring into our learning spaces and experiences should have a specific learning purpose as clutter can be disruptive to learning.

What can you remove to create opportunities that amplify learning?

How can you eliminate the distractions that affect learning?

5000 Sheets
20lb
8.5 x 11
Natural Choice
SCOTT FORESMAN
Space & Technology Science Unit
Grade 1
Qty: 1 Kit

WHAT DOES THE RESEARCH SAY:

"The visual complexity caused by an abundance of text and small images can set up an overwhelming visual/verbal competition between text and graphics for which students must gain control in order to give meaning to information."

Revisiting Your Classroom's Walls: The Pedagogical Power of Posters -Michael Hubenthal and Thomas O'Brien 2009

"Each feature of the architectural environment influences certain brain processes such as those involved in stress, emotion and memory."

Form Follows Function: Bridging Neuroscience and Architecture -Edelstein and Macagno 2012

".. By removing, or at least minimising visual noise, the visual system is freed up to concentrate on what's relevant or important making it easier for students to focus on the task at hand. Again, it is worth remembering here, that the best way to nudge the behaviour you want is to make it easy."

The Neuroscience of Classrooms- Dr Tim Holmes 2017

Coordinating color supports learning.

- By coordinating color we can minimize visual noise and create a lower-stress environment.

Declutter to support learning.

- Make sure that all objects in a space support learning.

Freeing up space opens up opportunities.

-By removing furniture, we can provide students with an area for them to design the learning spaces they need.

You <u>can</u> have too much of a good thing.

We all know what happens when a teacher leaves something out in the hallway with a "free" sign on it. But rarely do those free tables, cabinets, and stuff really meet the needs of our classroom.

Don't let resource scarcity be the designer of your space. Support your school to feel free to get rid of what isn't serving them without the fear of "What if I eventually need it?"

What to look out for:
- Walls: Is information unnecessary or repetitive?
- Furniture: Are tables stacked with unused materials? Are additional chairs and desks available or stored in the classroom?
- Curricular materials and manipulatives: Are there boxes that never get opened in a school year?

Support teachers to recognize what can go and what must stay.

ADDITION BY SUBTRACTION

What can you do without? What is preventing you from innovating?

✚ *Intentional Design*

Add elements that support learning, including items that promote discovery and curiosity. Stark spaces aren't the goal.

HOW TO SUPPORT TEACHERS:

Completely Empty the Space

And we mean everything. This is a great thing to do over an extended break. Once things are in the hallway or common space, they feel less necessary and it is easier to let go of what isn't serving your learners and your space. Not ready for the whole space? Try a closet or section of the classroom first.

Establish a Purgatory Space

Not sure about getting rid of something? Take it outside of the classroom. You can always bring it back in if it is needed. A closet or basement is a good option.

Be a Thought Partner

Simply asking, "Does this support learning?" or "How often does this support you?" is a good first step into going through a space. Stay away from accusatory tones or language and be there just as a support to help them re-frame how they look at the space and give permission to let go of stuff.

Offer to help

Roll up your sleeves or make that call to facilities yourself. This can feel very overwhelming when it is another thing added to teachers plates. Make it a one-hour release time, or forgo the faculty meeting and give teachers time to do this work.

ADDITION BY SUBTRACTION

Ask Students

When talking about the walls of the space, ask students what they truly notice and what is background noise. They know which elements are essential for instruction and which are superfluous.

Set Expiration Dates

How long is too long? Is it the best use of the space to have snowmen artwork up in April? Just like teachers set times for curricular goals, have them set goals for utilizing the vertical spaces (walls) in sync with current learning and instruction.

Define a wall of current learning

So it doesn't become a catch-all for anchor charts or past learning, have teachers set one wall in the space as focused on current instruction for the week. Essential questions, methods, and processes of learning can be highlighted and changed as a part of instruction.

Make it a monthly challenge

Have your teachers set a goal. Remove ten things each month and then reflect as a group.

As much as you can, let this be teacher-driven. Empower them to set goals for themselves, and then you can be their accountability partner.

Why it matters:
Push vs. Pull

The space can be a setting in which we push information at students or pull it through them. Empowering students as agents and owners of their learning allows teachers to break the direct instruction model and provides students with more opportunities for unique discovery. Our spaces can be rich with student-created artifacts and concepts instead of teacher-driven and/or purchased visuals.

How much information is being given to students versus how much is coming from their discoveries?

How can we provide powerful questions instead of answers to promote thinking?

Question Clouds

How do living things Survive and Thrive?

"I think I Know" Pond

How does the environment affect living things?

How do living things respond to their environment?

"I wonder" Lake

WHAT DOES THE RESEARCH SAY:

Student voice activities can create meaningful experiences for youth that help to meet fundamental developmental needs, especially for students who otherwise do not find meaning in their school experiences...this research finds a marked consistency in the growth of agency, belonging and competence -three assets that are central to youth development.

The significance of students: Can increasing "student voice" in schools lead to gains in youth development? -Dana Mitra 2004

....visible thinking has a diagnostic function. By providing a visible record of children's thinking, it allows teachers to see what students are learning and where they need help.

Visible Thinking- Shari Tishman and Patricia Palmer 2005

Display student work. Students not only feel a greater sense of responsibility for their learning but are also more likely to remember the material.

The Impact of Classroom Design on Pupils' Learning- Barrett et al., 2015

Students need to guide parts of the learning.

- Agency and choice in learning promote deeper engagement and satisfaction in learning.

Let thinking be visual.

- Drawing and sketching promote the transfer of ideas from working memory to long-term memory.

Create spaces for student voice.

- Where can you provide spaces to pull in students' feelings, ideas, and feedback so that co-creation is the norm of the learning space?

Providing space for students to discover, share, and lead

When you teach a child something, you take away forever his chance of discovering it for himself. - Piaget

Can our walls become the space where students' discoveries, inferences and learning comes alive? So often caring teachers fill their walls with information that quickly becomes invisible to the learners. Instead of pushing content at learners, provide them time and space to be the constructors of their learning.

Want to know who is doing the learning, check the artifacts:

- It is teacher-driven if the work looks the same, assignments and projects have the same outcome.
- It is learner-driven if the work is unique, has different outcomes and varied projects as well as evidence of personalization and thinking.

Support teachers to let go of the need to control.

PUSH VS. PULL

PUSH → TEACHER MADE / BOUGHT
(LECTURE, INFO)

PULL → STUDENT GENERATED
(I THINK THAT, WE DISCOVERED, HOW MIGHT WE..., OUR IDEAS)

HOW TO SUPPORT TEACHERS:

Look at the Walls

How much of the displayed information is being "pushed" at students or "pulled" through them? Just as teacher talk time is pushing content to students, classroom walls can also push content. Anchor charts, rules, and content-rich posters that already have all of the answers are pushing content toward students. (In many classrooms, the walls are a fire hydrant of pushed content.) This content push can actually have a negative effect by enabling students with this information and therefore limiting their time and opportunity to move it from short-term to long-term memory.

Define Co-construction Spaces

Use wall space, bulletin boards, and writable spaces as co-construction spaces where students are actively pulling together knowledge through recall, conversation, meaning-making, and the synthesis of ideas.

Emphasize Current Learning

Idea-rich classrooms that inspire communication and critical thinking are always looking for ways to thread knowledge together, create new meaning, and transfer ideas between situations. This is rarely possible when the facilitator pushes information through too much lecture or when all of the knowledge is pushed at students through the perimeter design of the learning space.

PUSH VS. PULL

Check the Artifacts

Do they reveal learners' unfolding ideas as they think through content and learning? Are they evidence of learning or heavily guided and controlled products?

Share Content in Other Ways

Can you place your large posters in folders that are easily accessible to students? Can you take photos and put them in a shared digital folder? Can you have word buckets instead of word walls?

Start Small

Try sharing your "push" materials in two or three ways. Then observe how students prefer to access the information so that you can design the space accordingly. Asking a student,"Which is the best way for you?" will help you make those decisions.

Be the Example

Use visible thinking strategies in your professional development. Check the hallways, office areas, and other shared spaces to be sure that you have the right push/pull balance for your culture.

We recommend not creating a specific ratio of push versus pull. Each space and need are unique. That type of thinking usually evokes compliance rather than commitment.

Why it matters:
Process over product

> Learning is a process, but too often our learning spaces showcase final product and undervalue the journey that it took to get there. Mistakes, struggle, and hard work lead to great learning. Allow your building to showcase discovery and the process of learning by breaking down each step of the learning experience into a variety of displays. Growth mindset is at the heart of "process over product."

What can we do in our learning spaces to show students that learning is a process filled with mistakes, drafts, and iteration?

How can we make our learning spaces showcase the importance of hard work in the learning process?

Meet William Kamkwamba

WHAT DOES THE RESEARCH SAY:

The processes of preparing and displaying documentaries of children's efforts provides a kind of re-visiting of experience during which new understandings are clarified and strengthened.

<u>The Contribution of Documentation to the Quality of Early Childhood Education</u>- Katz & Chard 1996

In this study, the researchers designed a broader system of tools that required students to publicly defend their designs earlier in the process. Requiring students to track and defend their thinking focused them on learning and connecting concepts in their design work.

<u>A case study of problem-based learning in a middle school science classroom</u> -Gertzman & Kolodner 1996

The findings of this research study suggest the benefits of the process writing approach in the studies of written expression. Students find writing activities more difficult than other language skills. Therefore, the obstacles to successful learning of writing skills should be accurately identified, and varied techniques should be used to eliminate them.

<u>The Effect of the Process Writing Approach on Writing Success and Anxiety</u> -Bayat 2014

Revision is key for excellence

- Provide time for students to return to their work so that they can continue to reflect and revise.

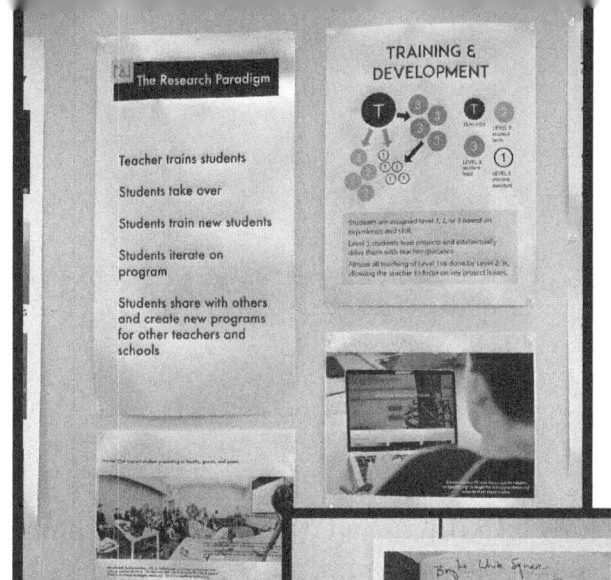

Provide feedback throughout the process

- Specific feedback that guides students to the next steps celebrates and nudges the process.

Display the process to showcase value

- Our walls tell a story about what matters. Let the hard work of learning be seen on the walls.

How can we see the learning unfold?

Why do we focus so much on the end products of learning? Probably, because they are so much easier to measure and evaluate than the process of learning. But it is by sharing and celebrating the process of learning that we provide insights into what is happening behind the scenes, and we make our thinking more visible.

There are many ways to allow our walls tell the whole story of our learning journeys.

Begin this work by having:

- Walls that show drafts and revisions
- Displays that make the learning process or problem solving process visible
- Spaces that share the "first we..." "then we..." "finally we..." and "next time we will..."

Ask yourself, Is what I am showcasing cultivating and celebrating growth over time or pressuring students through fear of public display?

PROCESS OVER PRODUCT

HOW TO SUPPORT TEACHERS:

Walls Focus on The Learning Journey

Allow more of the perimeter of your room to be student-designed and curated. When students are the curators, they can display what matters to them. This begins to tell their story of learning. Students can own the process when they are surrounded by it.

Assess the Learning Process

If you are just assessing and giving grades, then the message that the process is essential gets lost with traditional assessment. Look for quality ways to measure hard work and success throughout the learning.

Celebrate Risks

Continuing to see positive risks through the lens of what they discovered on this journey. There is learning in risk-taking, and it is important to model and discuss risk taking as a leader and teachers as well. Make these celebrations frequent and central to the learning.

Be the Example

Share your learning process. There is so much for students to learn by hearing the process of others. Students are looking for ways to learn that fit their style, but they rarely have examples that they can use to model their actions.

PROCESS OVER PRODUCT

Display Images of Process

When you add images of students doing the learning to the walls or the digital display in the room, you are reinforcing the importance of process and providing visual anchors to positive classroom behavior.

Use Growth Mindset Language

As students work on projects and assignments, there continues to be power in the use of the word YET. Students need to hear in frustrating moments that in their struggle, they are just not there YET.

Teach Design Processes

Learning how to learn can't be left to chance. Teach students the science behind learning, and equip them with processes for learning that transcend the subject matter and grade level. Take time to explicitly teach learning and design processes.

Display Shifting Ideas and Understanding

The beauty of a great classroom discussion is the unfolding of the thinking and evolution of ideas. Showcase this process using a writable surface in the room. This records how our thinking changes over time and shows us that our thinking can evolve, and change direction.

Why it matters:
Equity and Agency

Everyone wants a place of belonging. Unfortunately, we have systems, rules, and processes that both intentionally and unintentionally exclude and disenfranchise. It is our responsibility as leaders to make sure that the work to optimize learning spaces never goes a day without the lens of equity and the commitment to student agency being a central mindset. Too many learning space changes under-perform because the commitment to equity and agency simply go overlooked during the process.

What intentional design elements can you bring to the space to send a clear message that all are welcome to learn here?

How can students play a central role in the learning design, including what they learn, how they learn, and where they learn?

Where are you?

Art Studio

Tangerine Band Space

Bathr

Common

WHAT DOES THE RESEARCH SAY:

The researchers found that agentic engagement correlated with motivation, and that agentic engagement independently predicted student achievement.

<u>Agency as a Fourth Aspect of Students' Engagement during Learning Activities</u>- Reeve and Tseng 2011

Students from minority cultures may feel pressured to disavow themselves of their cultural beliefs and norms in order to assimilate into the majority culture. This, however, can interfere with their emotional and cognitive development and result in school failure.

<u>Relating Competence in an Urban Classroom to Ethnic Identity Development</u>- Sheets 1999

The promotion of individual agency may do little good if the larger community, such as a school or district, does not share the belief that agency is positive and productive.

<u>Teacher Agency: An Ecological Approach</u>- Biesta, Priestley & Robinson 2015

Culturally responsive education builds instructional practices around opportunities to process information in ways that makes learning sticky, then students become able to carry more of the cognitive load that leads to doing more rigorous work.

<u>Culturally Responsive Teaching and the Brain</u> - Hammond 2015

Agency supports motivation

- When students feel purpose in the work and a voice in crafting the journey, engagement rises.

If you can see it, you can be it.

- Spaces should celebrate the cultures and backgrounds of all students.

Space should welcome all learners

-Equitable spaces allow all students to feel welcome, safe, and supported based on their design.

How can you meet your students as individuals?

We want to empower our students. We want to build digital and physical spaces in which they are self-driven learners. But time and time again we allow myths of the lack of student engagement in our historically under-served students to justify our inaction.

We are not experts in social justice issues. We highly recommend digging into this work with your school by studying the work of Zaretta Hammond, Ibram X Kendi, Chris Emdin, Lisa Delpit and organizations like the National Equity Project. This work cannot be left to chance.

What to look out for:

- Create a space that is psychologically safe for staff, faculty, families and learners to share their opinions and voices.
- Ensure your design teams represent all cultures in your community.
- Shape your spaces to enhance students' natural learning strengths and connect content and rituals to students' lives.

Support teachers to recognize what can go and what must stay.

EQUITY AND AGENCY

WE ALL HAVE A VOICE

HOW TO SUPPORT TEACHERS:

Choice in How and Where Students Learn

Do you know how and where you learn best? How did you learn? When did you learn? Were you given a chance to figure it out in a low-stakes environment where you have lots of opportunities to try? This is a career goal for our students. Give them space and time in this area.

Design a Questioning Environment

What are the essential questions that you are exploring? Are they visible and prominent in your space? Questions can emerge from discovery and exploration as well. How does your space allow for both of these key learning actions to happen?

Classroom Represents Culture

Designing a culturally responsive classroom includes thinking about the words and images that you display in the learning space. It isn't about simply adding, but thinking about proportionality as well. Many educators can over-correct in this area, so take time to be deeply thoughtful about your design and continue to have it evolve as the students you serve change over time.

Think about Trauma Informed Design

More and more students are learning with the impact of trauma as a part of their lives. Our learning space design should be responsive, including a space to decompress without leaving the instructional, a design that allows for class meetings, and a model of open-ended questions that mirror trauma-informed support of students.

EQUITY AND AGENCY

Explore Implicit Bias

All humans have absorbed data and gathered observations in our lives that have created bias in our thinking. If we can surface this truth, there is a chance to counteract bias based on inertia and begin to reshape the little things that make a big impact on our students and their learning.

Students as Co-Designers

Students should definitely have a voice around how the classroom space can support their learning, but this co-designer status shouldn't end with the arrangement of the room. What else can you include students in?

Psychological Safety

Do students feel like they are free to share things that scare them without fear of recriminations or negative social pressure? Classrooms designed to promote this level of safety help students have powerful, transformative conversations. Shape your space to promote this reality.

Seek Social Justice Conversations

When students feel as though they have to be silent about the injustices that they notice around them, it can inhibit their will to act. Speak out when you notice these things in the world. The space, both literal and figurative, can motivate us to action.

Welcome to the end of the beginning

At this point, you should be more confident. You have team armed with purpose and mindsets, and you are ready to start making changes that have a lasting impact.

WHY LEADERS CONSIDER SPACE

IMPACT OF SPACES

HOW SPACE AFFECTS CULTURE

PURPOSEFUL DESIGN

LEARNING SPACE MINDSETS

A cluttered mind struggles to have a vision for what is possible.

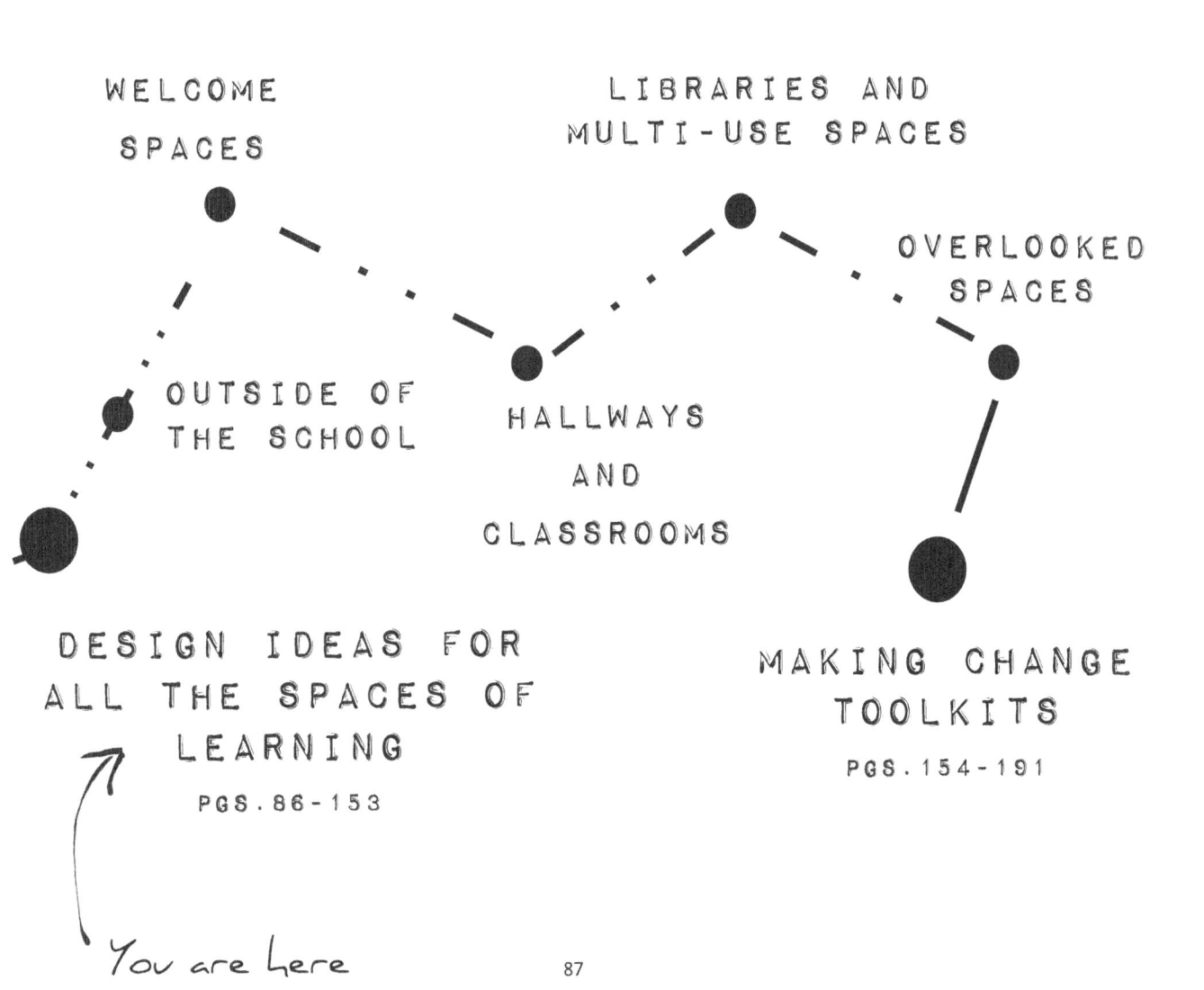

WELCOME SPACES

LIBRARIES AND MULTI-USE SPACES

OVERLOOKED SPACES

OUTSIDE OF THE SCHOOL

HALLWAYS AND CLASSROOMS

DESIGN IDEAS FOR ALL THE SPACES OF LEARNING

PGS. 86-153

MAKING CHANGE TOOLKITS

PGS. 154-191

You are here

Let's take a design journey through the whole building.

WELCOME SPACES

THE OUTSIDE OF SCHOOL

HALLWAYS

The culture of your school is what drives the choices you make in how your school looks and feels.

LIBRARIES AND MULTI-USE SPACES

CLASSROOMS

OVERLOOKED SPACES

THE OUTSIDE OF THE SCHOOL

WHAT ARE
THE OPPORTUNITIES?

Purposeful signage and clean landscaping begins to tell a story about what matters, and how well we care for kids.

What to expect...

- Playgrounds and athletic fields should feel like community spaces, but mirror the messaging about the culture and learning inside.
- Language on signs should be mission- focused.
- The outdoor experience should reinforce the thoughtful, intentional design on the inside of the building.

Most community members never get an opportunity to visit the inside of your school.

The outdoor of the school shapes what they imagine learning looks like on the inside.

MENLO PARK ACADEMY

THE OUTSIDE OF SCHOOL

WHAT ARE THE CONSIDERATIONS?

The spaces around the exterior of the building tell a non-verbal story. They are the first impression that many have when they visit the school. Signage, accessibility, and landscaping can play a role in launching learning from outside in.

First Steps:

- Ask someone from the community to share their lens.
- Notice the space in new ways.
- Consider the words, logos and symbols on the exterior.
- Make a habit of walking around the perimeter of the building to gain a fresh perspective.

Reality Check: There are many vintages of buildings, and some have greater street appeal. Optimize what you have as the building itself speaks loudly about the mission.

What about this entrance?

Is this a community space?

Opportunity for learning?

What does this say?

view from the street?

THE OUTSIDE OF SCHOOL

Creating a Sense of Belonging

John Eick, Westlake Charter School (CA)

Why did you focus on the outside of the building ?

As a school, we had been moving from temporary space to temporary space for a number of years, and when we moved to our permanent space, we knew that we had a unique opportunity for intentionality. We worked to make our entire campus an inspirational space for learning, beginning from the first step on campus.

Where did you find success?

Since the move to our current space, teachers throughout our entire organization have begun the release of ownership to whom, it really belongs to: the students. We are now seeing the multi-year effects of this shift as students take ownership over more than simply where they sit.

What other learning came from the project?

Honest dialogue with students is essential to good learning choices. We have supported students in their journey to learn where they learn best, both in the classroom and throughout the campus, and now self-reflective behaviors are more observable at every grade level.

What advice would you give others working on similar things?

Leave no space behind. The story about our school begins each day with the families and community members that drive by our school. They can tell from the design that something amazing is happening on the inside.

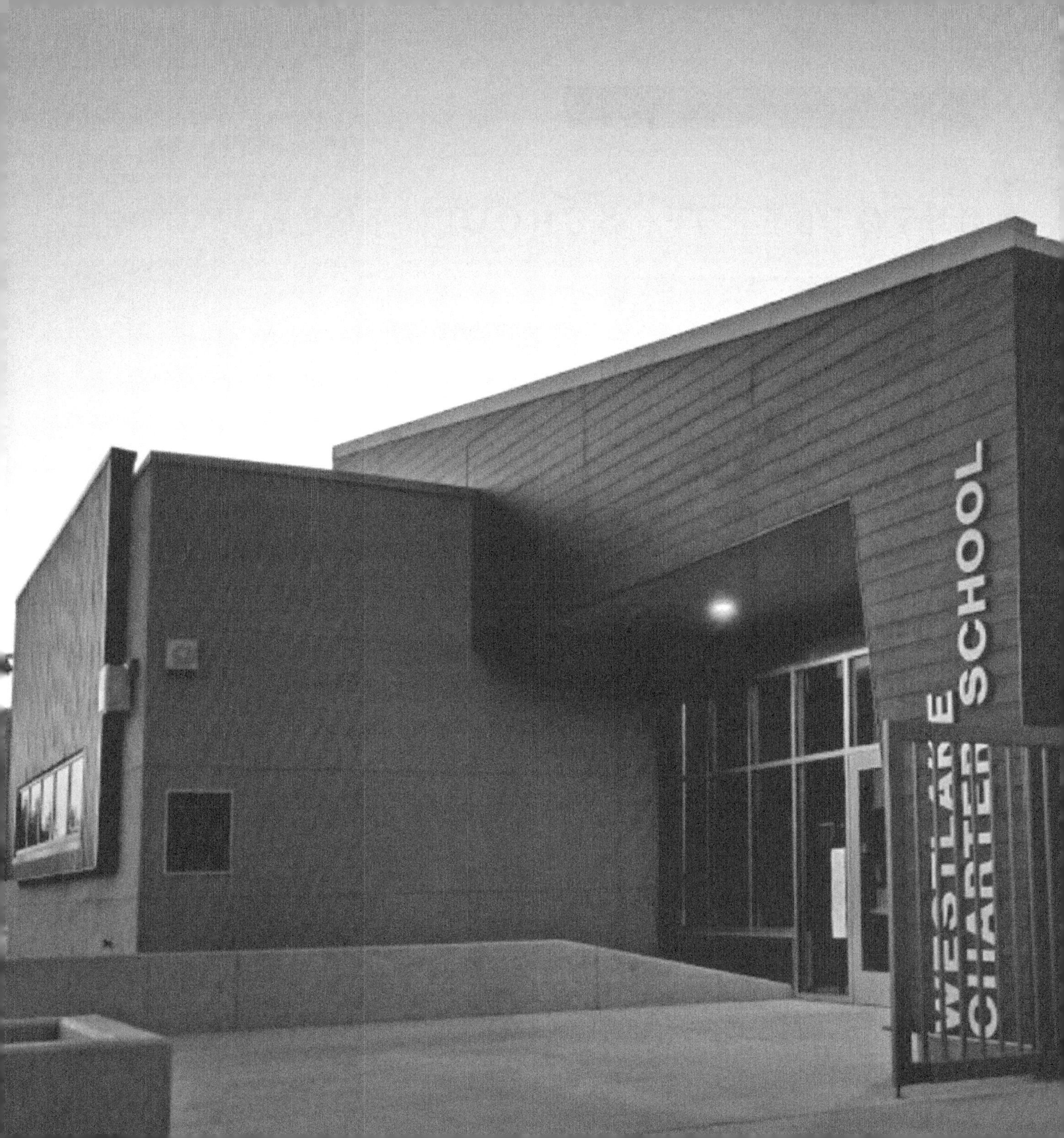
CHARTER
SCHOOL

THE OUTSIDE OF SCHOOL

OUTSIDE OF SCHOOL IDEAS

TRY IT TODAY
Change Your Signage

Make it a message that inspires and draws people into the building. Everyone who sees your sign should know what you care about.

(This is as much for the community as it is for your learners.)

ALSO THIS
Mission Forward

Do visitors feel the mission from the outside of your building? Do families know that you want them inside? Is there an energy that attracts people inside? Language, color, and signage play a role in creating a welcoming atmosphere.

OR EVEN THIS
Window Debris

Develop school norms about what can be seen in classroom windows. Too often, this is left to chance, and it sends a message that dated, faded, and damaged have replaced excellence in the school.

(Take the staff on a perimeter walk of the school. Pay particular attention to the items that you can see from the window and what message they are sending.)

OR MAYBE
Enhance the Green Space

If the grass, plants, and trees are maintained and showcase a sense of design, it sends a message that order and peace are inside as well. Make it a norm that trash, extra items, and leaves are maintained.

WELCOME SPACES - ENTRY OF BUILDING

WHAT ARE
THE OPPORTUNITIES?

Welcoming people into a space is an essential element in crafting a positive culture. Images of students' learning and intentional language on signs can make a great first impression. The entrance speaks loudly, and when well designed, sparks an initial energy for learning.

Questions to ask...

- Have we avoided the word "no" being a part of the entrance experience?
- How is your entrance a mini-experience of the overall school? (How close is the learning?)
- Can your entrance better welcome those marginalized by school systems?

Students, teachers, and family members are introduced to the mission and vision of a school each day when they walk through the entrance. What messages are you sending?

Learn more about Brightworks School at sfbrightworks.org

WELCOME SPACES- ENTRY OF BUILDING

WHAT ARE THE CONSIDERATIONS?

"Enter at your own risk" shouldn't be the impression. The entrance should be a place of healthy gathering that welcomes all no matter their readiness, desire to be there, or comfort with the school. It can be the energy catalyst for everyone every day.

First Steps:

- Add art and images of students
- Limit text-rich signs and notices
- Help people see that they have arrived in a place that is different from most spaces for learning

Reality Check: Some schools have a multitude of entry points to their campus. You may have to spread your resources across many locations. Develop a coherent, strategic plan.

Is this a hiding place?

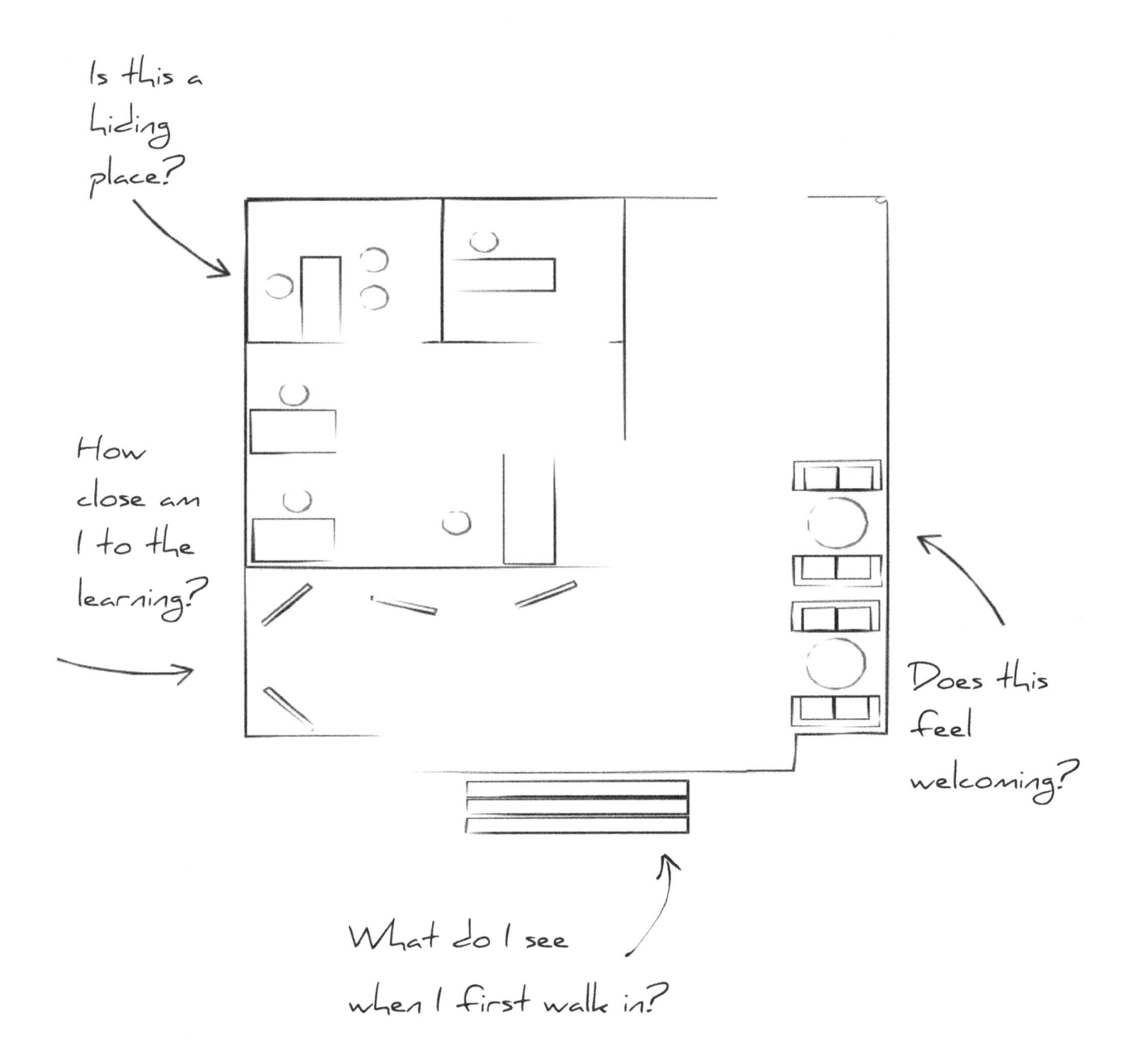

How close am I to the learning?

Does this feel welcoming?

What do I see when I first walk in?

`WELCOME SPACE- ENTRY OF BUILDING`

AS YOU ENTER SCHOOL...

`TRY IT TODAY`

Breaking the Mental Model

What is the first impression that visitors get as they walk into the school? Does it let them know that modern learning is different? Let them see coherent visuals, avoid unpleasant noises and smells, and begin their experience with a smile and positive energy.

`ALSO THIS`

Images of Learning

Move images of the modern learning happening in classrooms as close to the entrance as possible. Visitors that never make it to the classroom should have an accurate look at the learning.

`OR EVEN THIS`
Safety Through Hospitality

Humans feel safe when they feel belonging and welcoming into a space. Buzzers, locked doors, and metal detectors could be your entry way reality, but it is the first person that greets someone that gives the most powerful impression of safety, comfort, and care.

`OR MAYBE`
Reduce the Noise

Entering a school building can be overwhelming. Signs about everything impact nothing. Help people know where to go and aid them in getting a sense of mission and purpose through more images and less text.

WELCOME SPACES - THE OFFICE

WHAT ARE THE OPPORTUNITIES?

Those that enter the office should leave with more energy instead of less. They should see signs that the school is efficient and effective with its systems. The office should showcase the desire of the school to be orderly.

Begin with...

- Reducing the visual noise throughout the office.
- Making sure the learning mission is visible in text and images.
- Updating items that are damaged or faded.
- Building in time to tidy up and move items to storage or recycling.

Spaces that stay messy, busy, and devoid of energy can reflect on the work of those who inhabit the spaces. Intentionally build in the time to maintain them so that they don't spiral out of control.

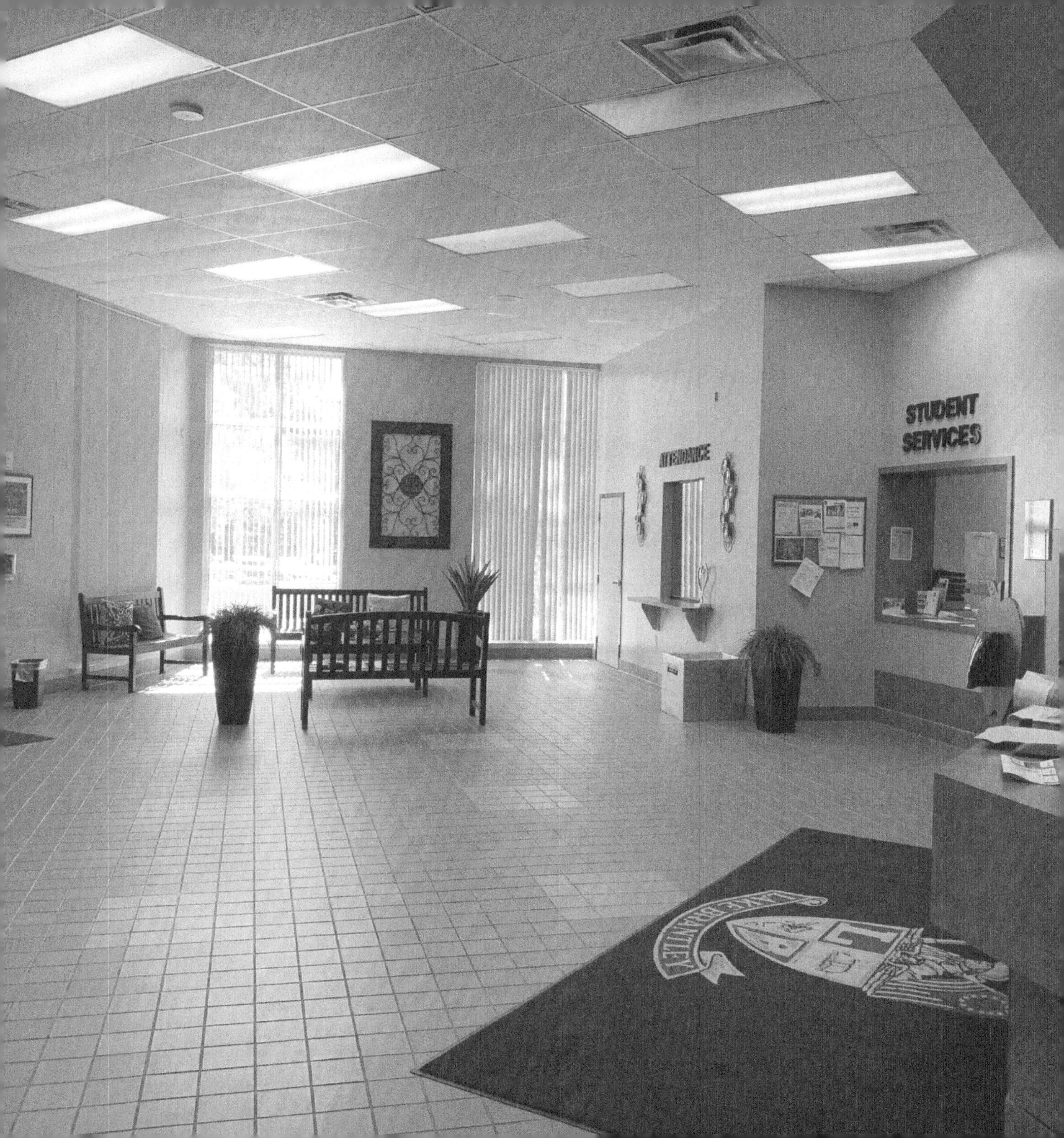
STUDENT
SERVICES
LAKE BRANTLEY

WELCOMING SPACES- THE OFFICE

MESSAGES FROM THE OFFICE

TRY IT TODAY
A Hero's Welcome

The best school office environments welcome people as though they have arrived for a great feast at someone's home. They say, "We're glad you're here, and we want your visit to be in an incredible one."

ALSO THIS
Don't Lead with the Sheet

Too many visitors encounter sign-in sheets and stoic faces when they enter school offices; they feel like a burden before they have even said hello.

`OR EVEN THIS`

Clearly define Storage Etiquette

The collection of stuff can overwhelm an office space, and it speaks to the type of school where the visitor has arrived. Let the message of the school say we pay attention to detail, and it begins with how we organize the office.

`OR MAYBE`

Overcome the Last Impression

Many school visitors don't have positive feelings about schools in general. Let their time in the office begin to peel back their past impressions and begin a new way of thinking about schools. Don't make them sit in the same seats as students waiting for discipline.

HALLWAYS

WHAT ARE
THE OPPORTUNITIES?

Allow hallways to contribute to learning and go beyond a series of bulletin boards with student work. It can expand the classroom by adding space to gather and collaborate.

Optimal hallways often include:

- furnishings that allow for students to sit or stand comfortably.
- interactive materials that create windows into the learning.
- writable spaces that utilize the walls as place of drawing and sketching so thinking can be visualized.
- showcases of learning that include images of the learner in process.

Hallway challenges are a great to way to get student voice and ideas into the process. Identify five or so areas in hallways that are underutilized and need updates, create a contest for small groups of students to redesign these spaces.

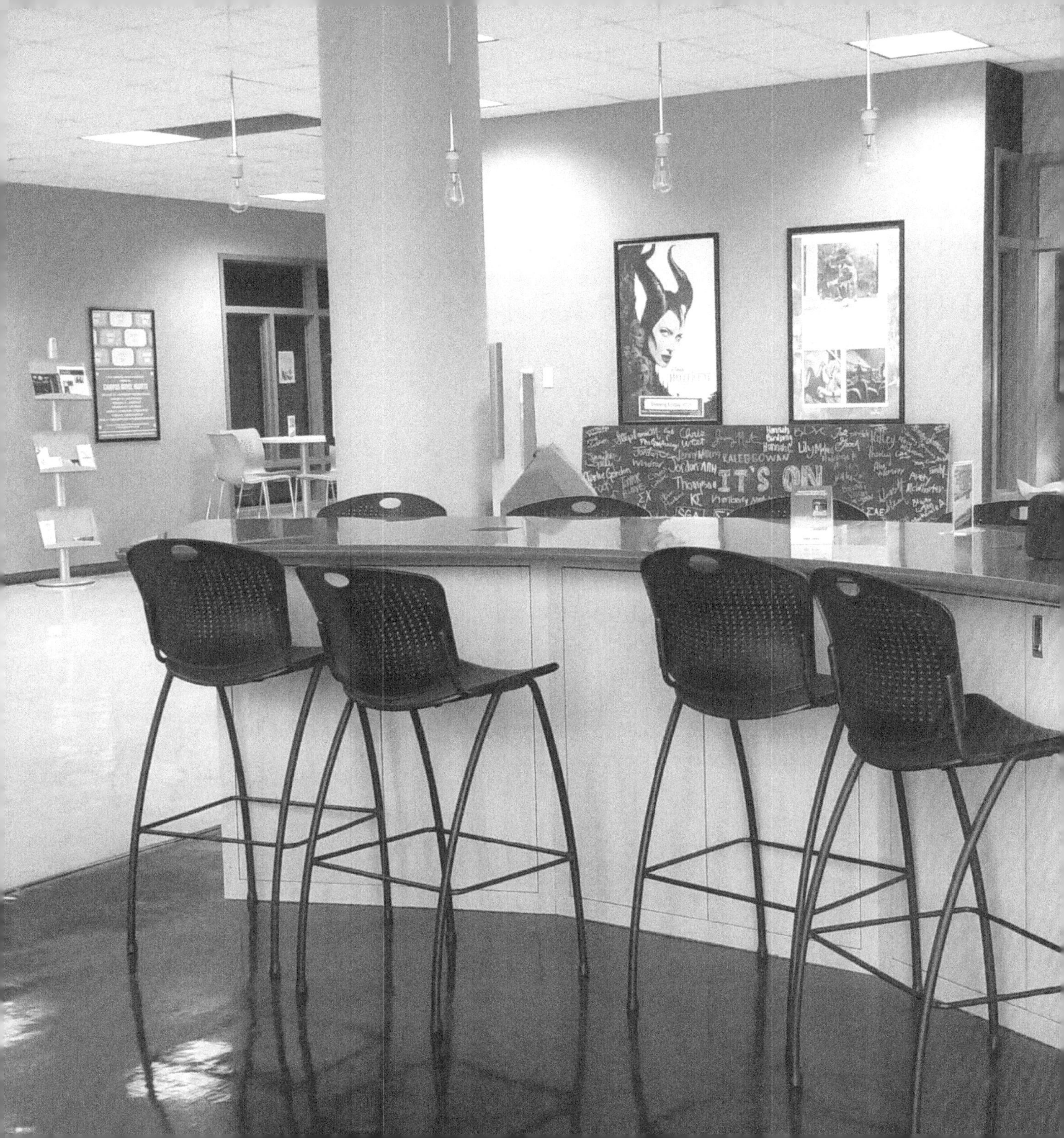
IT'S ON

HALLWAYS

WHAT ARE THE CONSIDERATIONS?

Almost one-third of the square feet of most schools is hallway space, and it has historically been an afterthought as a space. All spaces need to be be learning spaces, so consider the hallway as an extension of the classroom and a way to unify the learning mission throughout the building.

First Steps:

- Create opportunities for students to explore and discover in the hallways.
- Have signage that describes the history and science of the building, so that students make connections.
- Design displays that celebrate hard work and showcase learning as a process.
- Develop ways for students to physically interact with the hallway, including prompts on the floor and walls.

Reality Check: Hallways without intentional design can be dark and devoid of positive stimulus. Don't let the hallways become energy vampires.

Do the hallways reflect your mission?

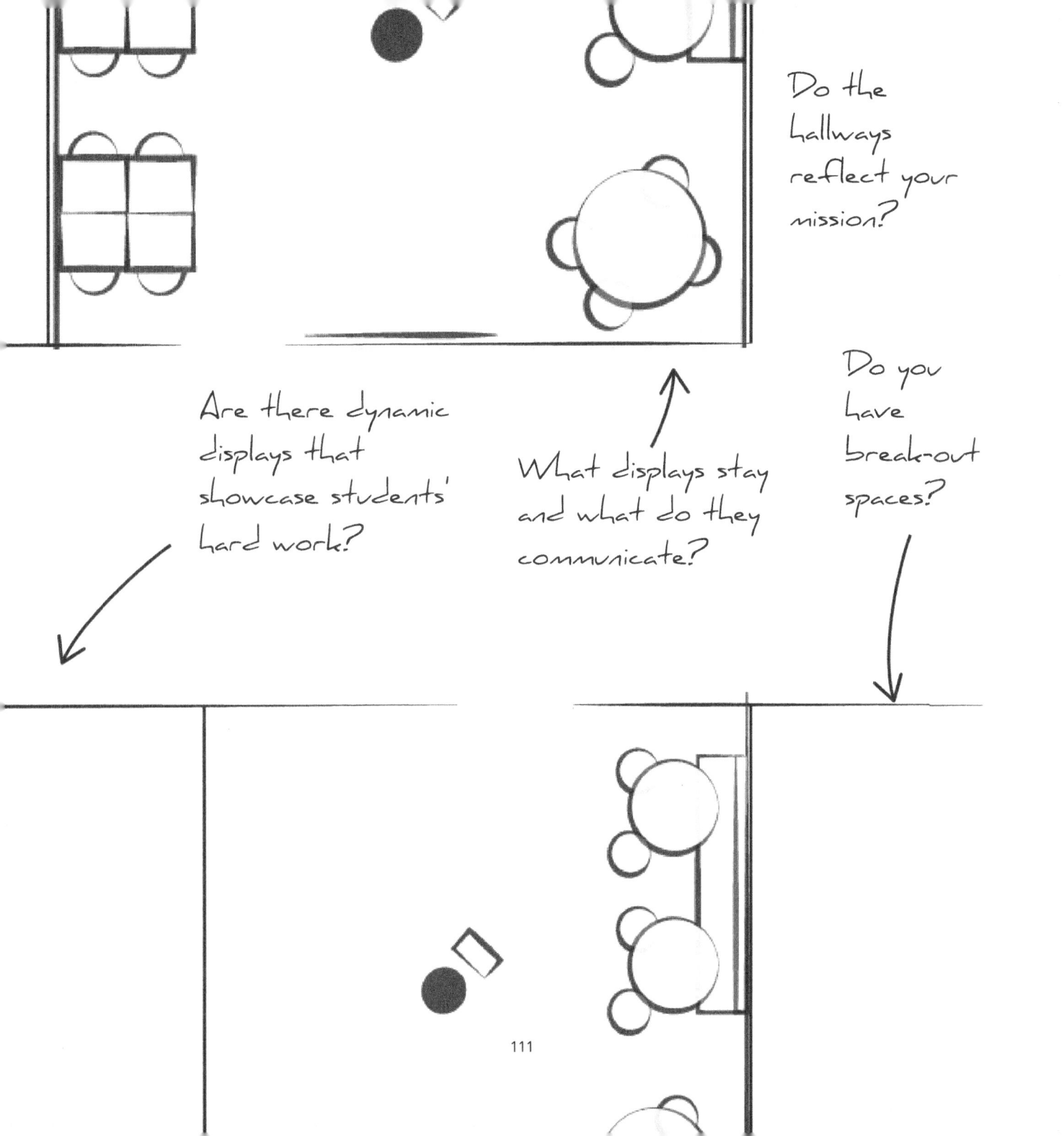

Are there dynamic displays that showcase students' hard work?

What displays stay and what do they communicate?

Do you have break-out spaces?

HALLWAYS

Expanding the Spaces for Learning

Patrick R. Keenoy, Rogers Elementary School

Why did you have a focus on your hallways?

Including our hallways as a piece of our learning space journey was intended to grow the positive culture of our school community and helped to bring about joy in learning. It also showcased the hard work and talent of our students reinforcing our desire for a strong community of learners.

Where did you find success?

Our journey in learning space design has brought about many positive attributes for our school community. One positive attribute has been a shift in culture, going from a culture of "me" to a culture of "we." This shift in mindset has resulted from the conversations occurring between teachers and students, as well as students engaging with one another.

What other learning came from the project?

These conversations about all spaces have given everyone a sense of ownership, of learning, and a feeling that we are all in this learning adventure together.

What advice would you give others working on similar things?

By providing students choice and voice in the design of the learning space, they have been more engaged in their learning. Allow students to be co-designers of hallways and classrooms as it provides students the chance to develop the skills of sharing, cooperation, problem-solving, and decision-making.

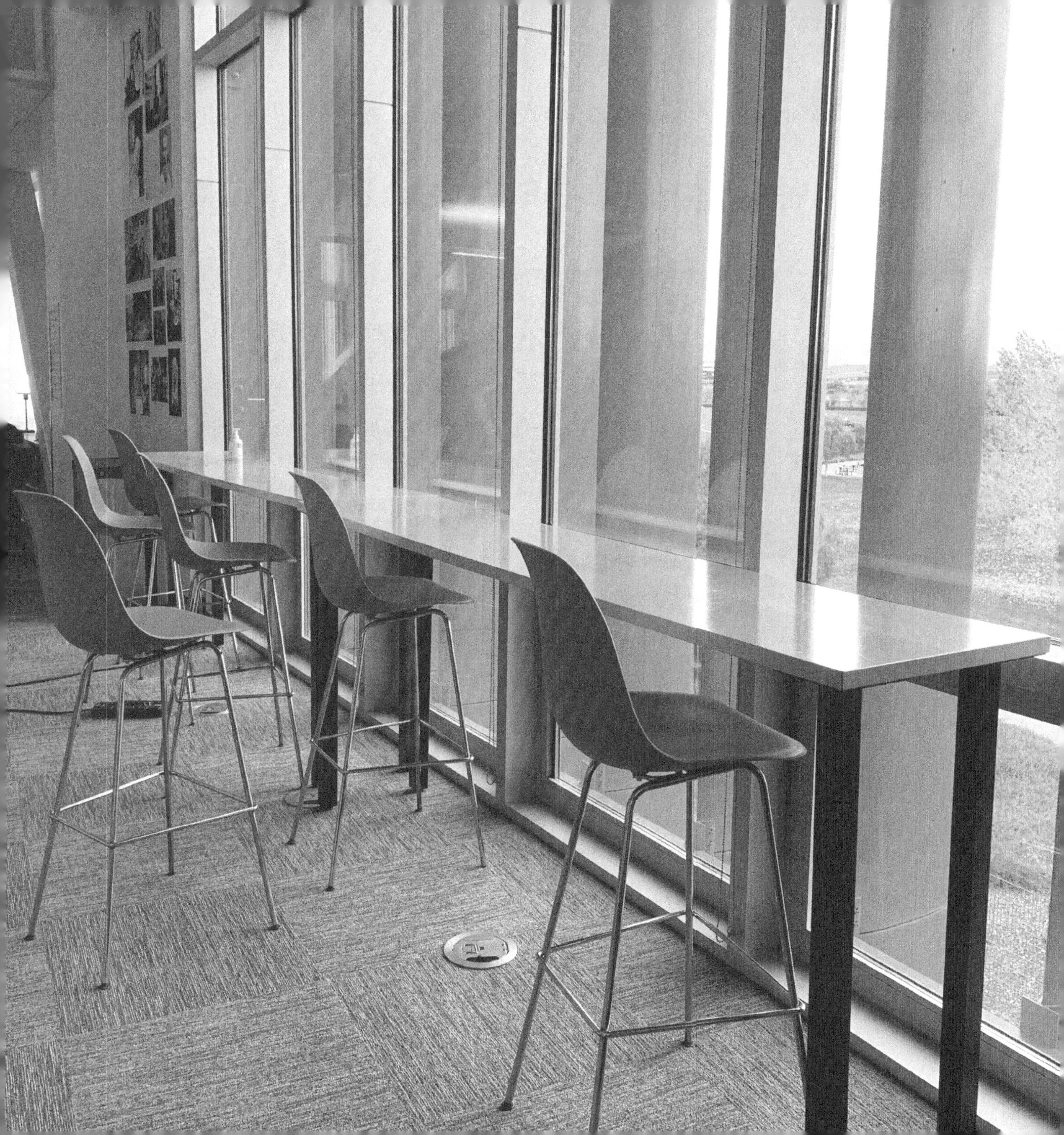

HALLWAYS

DESIGNING EVERY SQUARE FOOT

TRY IT TODAY
Draw the Learning Out

Make space for learning to spill out of the classroom. A few tables and seats will nudge collaboration to the hallway.

ALSO THIS:
Inspire with Art

The hallways have an opportunity to inspire. Consider the art, artifacts, and text that covers the walls. Look for overlooked spaces, like water fountain alcoves, and let art live outside of the bulletin board.

OR EVEN THIS
Have a Display Strategy

There could be static, dynamic, and digital displays in many hallways. Design them to tell a story, and have a plan on how to keep the content fresh and focused on the purpose of display.

OR MAYBE
Learning Everywhere

Let the hallways showcase unique aspects of the school. Signage that talks about the science that makes the building run and the history of the building and the land upon which it resides can be great hallway content.

CLASSROOMS

WHAT ARE
THE OPPORTUNITIES?

Classroom changes are often a catalyst for building-wide changes. These shifts in design empower teachers to craft a space that brings out their best work, and it allows them to feel safe to take positive risks for kids.

What to expect...

- Space that supports modern pedagogical practices.
- Spaces that bring increase engagement and students' satisfaction around their learning.
- Space that breaks the mental model of what a classroom has to be and allows educators to experience what is possible.

Classrooms are the biggest opportunity to impact student growth, but inertia and tradition can make this the hardest and scariest work.

Every child is an artist.
— PABLO PICASSO

CLASSROOMS

WHAT ARE
THE CONSIDERATIONS?

In classroom design, there are three basic ingredients to consider: mindset (what you value in learning experiences and how that will play out in the space), perimeter (the walls and boundaries of the space), and layout (how you set up the elements within the space). Layout also includes anchored elements such as built-in storage, closets, and demo stations (these are usually elements that you cannot change but could re-imagine).

First Steps:
- What cannot be changed?
- What can be changed?
- What can be re-imagined?

Reality Check: We know that there are inherent limitations to each space. Focus on what you can control right now.

What are the boundaries?

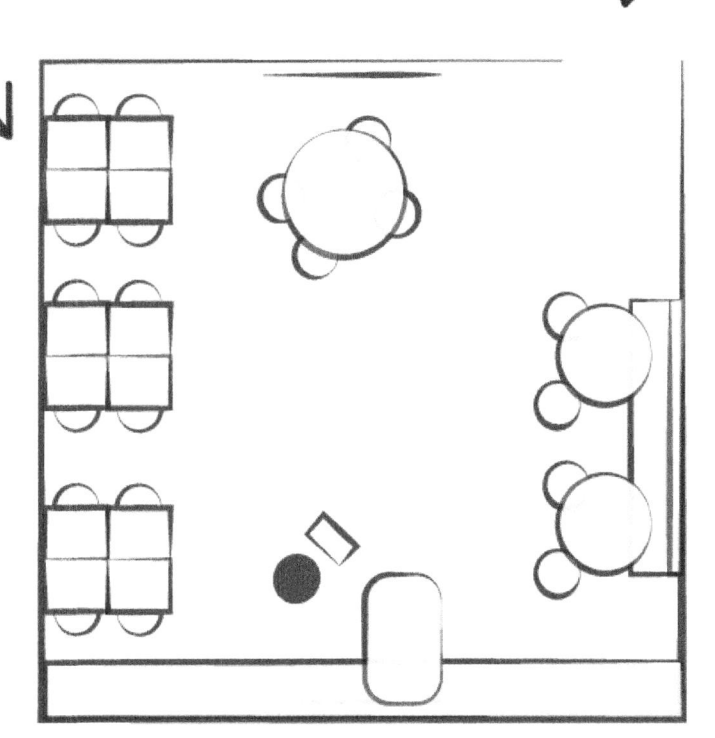

What types of elements are best for your space?

What is fixed and what can you re-imagine?

CLASSROOMS

How to Choose Stuff

We can easily get enamored with some new piece of furniture and then when we bring it into the space, it doesn't really solve our problems. Instead, start with thinking through the best descriptors of what you need to help you find the right stuff at the right budget. Here's how:

JUST RIGHT LANGUAGE

This is what you need to best describe what you want in your space. When we are imprecise with the description of what we need, we could end up with the wrong things in our space. Just right language is detailed enough to narrow down what we need, but not too detailed that we exclude other possible solutions.

Determine: Specific Functional Characteristics
- What is the function of the element?
- Who is it for?
- What should it do?
- How many will you need?
- What doesn't it need to do?
- What could it do next? (when your needs change)

(Because sometimes, when we define things well we realize that we already have it.)

THE GOLDILOCKS PRINCIPLE

Try using this ↙

To get your "just right language" precisely describe what you need for your space.

We need three tables.

TOO VAGUE

We need horizontal work surfaces that accommodates three groups of four to six students for collaborative writing and brainstorming.

Ideally, these would change height and be easy to move, maybe even store away. (could eventually be used for commons area for events)

JUST RIGHT

We need three seventy-inch tables with a hydraulic lift, and gray legs with white tabletops.

TOO SPECIFIC

CLASSROOMS

Elements within the Space

Each classroom will need something a little different based on size, development level of students, and environmental elements. But, they will most likely include some combination of: work surfaces, seating, storage and a teacher workstations. Here are some criteria to consider for each of these elements.

WORK SURFACES

An ideal student work surface should be agile (able to be re-configured according to learning needs and instructional models), and accommodate multiple activities.

We recommend choosing a variety of work surfaces at three heights (standing, sitting, lower floor/coffee table)

- Standing height surfaces allow students to build and do regular school work while moving and stretching.
- Seated height surfaces allow for rest while working and for making. and drawing.
- Lower height surfaces allow students to do work while in a non-traditional posture.

First: Choose simple shapes

○ △ ■ ▨

Can be tricky (triangle)

Then: Height(s)

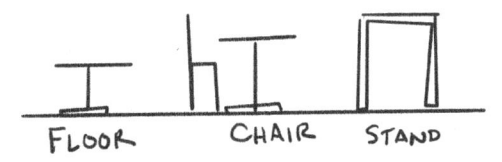

Floor — Chair — Stand

Finally: What else is needed?

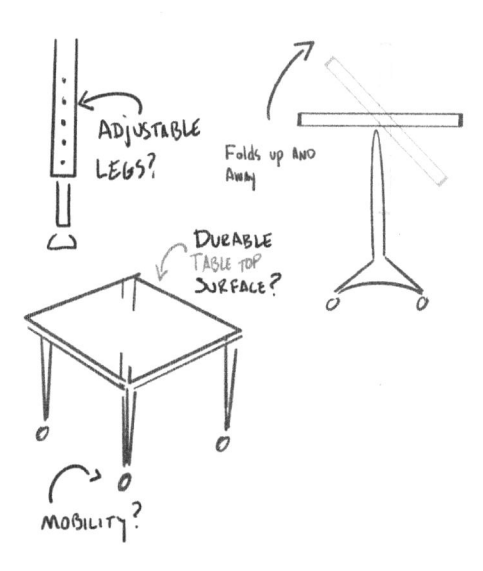

Adjustable legs?
Folds up and away
Durable table top surface?
Mobility?

The simplest shapes have the maximum agility: rectangles, squares, circles and some triangles (Beware of acute angles because kids cannot spread out learning materials).

WORK SURFACES TO CONSIDER:

- triangle desks for multiple configurations
- adjustable height desks & tables
- desks that stack
- tables with castors
- tall skinny tables to go under windows
- high-quality whiteboard surfaces
- tables that fold

DON'T WASTE TIME WITH:

- attached desks and chairs
- low-quality whiteboard surfaces.
- novel shapes, like commas, waves, etc.

CLASSROOMS

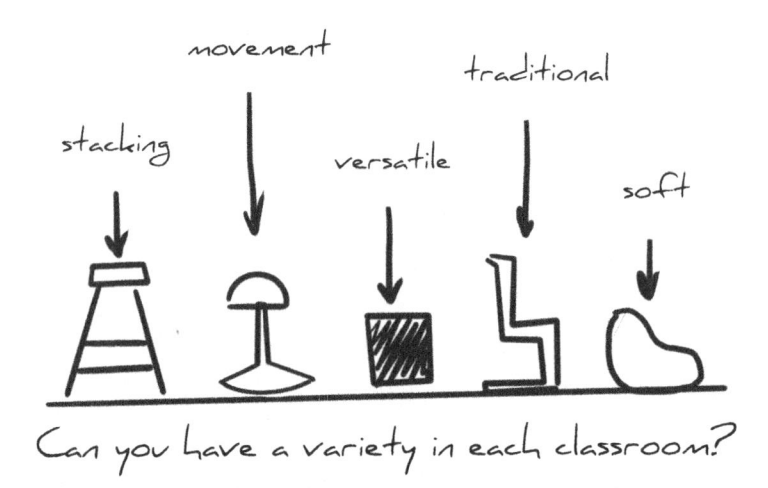

stacking · movement · versatile · traditional · soft

Can you have a variety in each classroom?

SEATING

Offering a variety of seating options helps students change posture throughout the day to increase vestibular stimulation, comfort and choice.

We recommend at least three different types of seating support in each classroom.

- Traditional chairs that can be stacked and be put away
- Comfortable casual seating (bean bags, armchairs, poufs)
- Stools or non-back-supporting seating that requires students to "lean-in." (These can be pushed under tables when not in use.)

SEATING TO CONSIDER

- Easy-to-move ottomans that can stack for students to lean against or lie over
- Balance chairs or stools
- Stackable chairs with backs
- Floor/lower relax-type seating
- Carpets for low tables and to work on the floor
- Soft stadium-type seating for direct instruction and for independent work in which students can find a variety of natural positions

*Depending on space availability, having 30% more seating options than students (39 options for a 30 student class or 26 options for a 20-student class) is the aim to provide choice. This does not mean extra chairs, it might be a just adding some pillows or a carpet area.

Doors are even better when they are writable

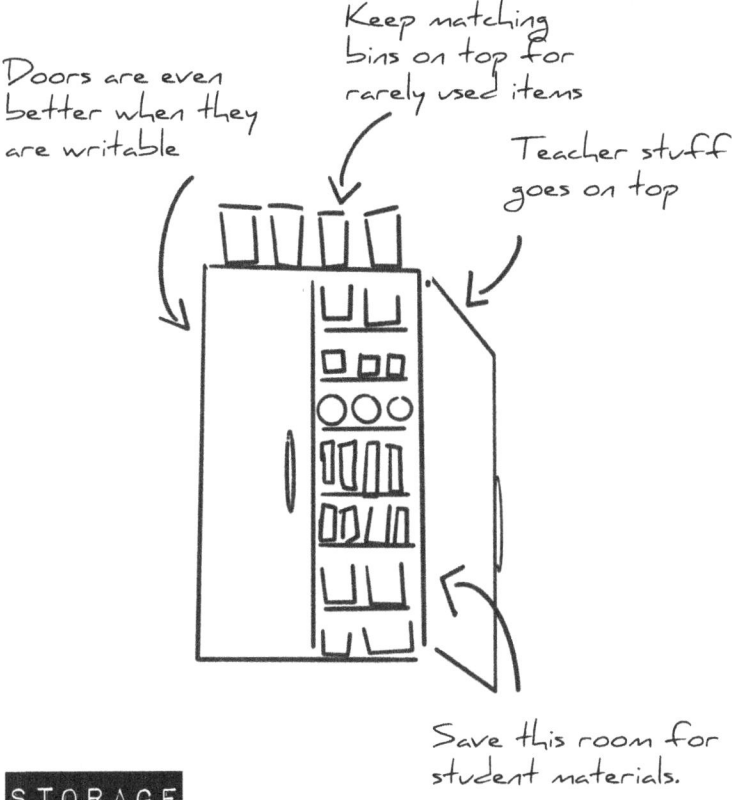

Keep matching bins on top for rarely used items

Teacher stuff goes on top

Save this room for student materials.

STORAGE

Storage is all about height. Who needs to get in it and when? Don't let your best storage real estate be filled with things you only use once in a while.

Student Storage Needs:

- A place for student belongings that support home/school transitions (accessed less frequently)
- A space for students to keep their supplies for work at school. (higher frequency of use, accessible and distributed throughout the room to avoid long lines)

Room Storage Considerations:

- Maximize the use of the vertical space (i.e. tall cabinets) to keep the impact of the storage at minimum.

STORAGE TO CONSIDER

- Tall storage cabinets with writable surfaces
- Mobile supply carts
- Storage under work spaces (especially for standing-height "makerspace" areas)
- Taller shelves or cabinets for materials that are seldom used
- Matching storage containers for manipulatives and classroom libraries
- Storage for student belongings (backpacks) at heights accessible to students

*Ideally, fronts of storage cabinets can be writable or used for display.

Seldom-used materials and teacher supplies can be kept at the top while more frequently used materials are on lower shelves.

CLASSROOMS

Mobile unit
Fixed work-station

Curves: can a work-surface be friendly?

How much space is teacher only?

TEACHER WORKSTATIONS

How much space should be teacher only space? Think about what you do in the space: present, facilitate, assess and get the right items that help you do that.

We recommend:

- A mobile unit (small podium that can wheel anywhere in the classroom to break the habits of teaching from the front)
- A fixed work station that has a small footprint for emails, grading, document camera, etc.

Horseshoe tables for small group instruction take up a lot of space in the room and are fixed. Using smaller student tables in a "U" or the floor can free up that much-needed space.

ITEMS TO CONSIDER

- A workspace with a small footprint
- A counter-height or standing workspace
- A cart, podium, or basket that has what you need when and wherever you need it
- A chair that goes from regular to counter height
- Secure lockable storage (Maybe you already have it somewhere else?)

IDEAS AND HABITS YOU COULD BREAK

- Having a teacher "desk"
- Being plugged-in (could you un-tether yourself from the front and present from the middle of the room?)
- Having a mini-kitchen (Is there a common space you could use where you can connect with other educators?)
- Can all spaces be "our" space? (could you break the hierarchy and be on "their" level?)

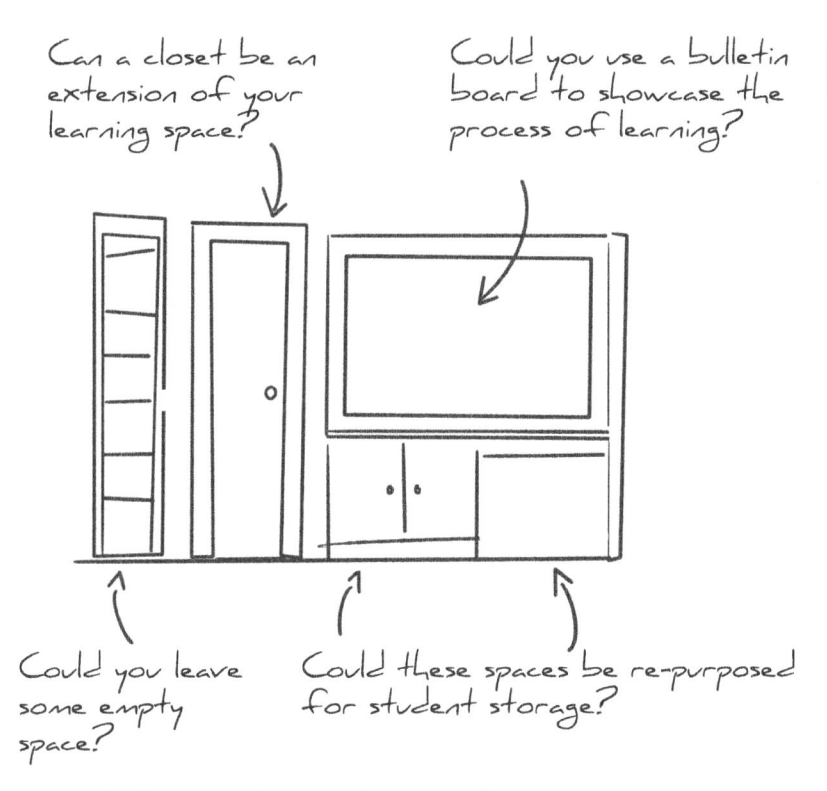

Can a closet be an extension of your learning space?

Could you use a bulletin board to showcase the process of learning?

Could you leave some empty space?

Could these spaces be re-purposed for student storage?

RE-PURPOSE ANCHORED ELEMENTS

What can you re-imagine and re-purpose to help your space become what you need?

Things ripe for re-purposing:

- Counters: These tend to collect papers and clutter but are great work surfaces. You can easily add a table top to expand the size.
- Window ledges: Add a thin table at the same height in front to connect to natural light.
- Closets and cabinets: Get rid/move seldom used materials to create nooks for reading or quiet mindfulness.

What other element changes could re-vitalize your space?

IDEAS TO CONSIDER

- Creating work surfaces around the perimeter of the room frees up space in the middle for more active learning
- Using a fixed-counter as a teacher workstation eliminates a big desk (and works as a free standing desk)
- Covering cabinets with shiny writable material for students to visualize their thinking and collaborate.
- Removing doors on lower cabinets to make these spaces more accessible and welcoming to students.

*To get started, have your students brainstorm all the ways they might be able to use the space (clear it off first). Try out a few of the ideas and let it evolve with intention.

CLASSROOMS

The Perimeter

Each classroom has some sort of boundary that defines it. Some are physical like walls, windows, cabinets, and doors, and some are habits that we define for safety, organization, institutional requirements, and legacy.

WALLS

We consider walls to be solid and opaque and the best real estate in your classrooms. We don't get to choose the size or material but we do get to choose what we do with the walls that are provided. Let's break down their use into two main categories:

Semi-Static:

- A place to provide information that is continuous and referenced often. (calendar, homework, schedules, etc.)

Dynamic:

- Space that is used to share information that is only necessary for a short time (one class, or one unit).
- A place to display student work, examples, and process.
- A place for students to make their thinking big. (writable surfaces dedicated to students, large pieces of paper, etc.)

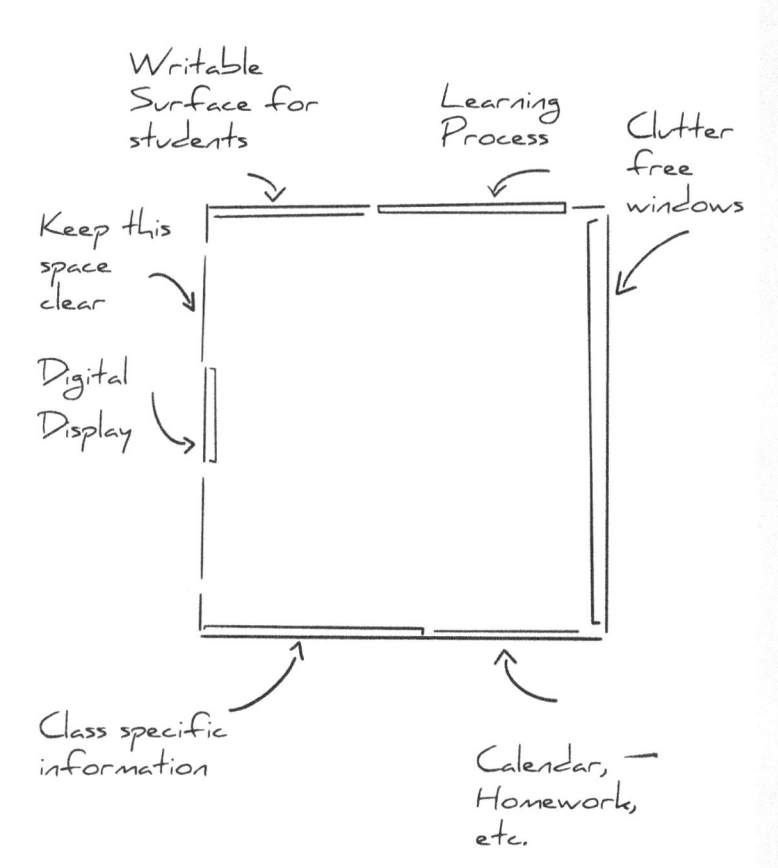

Diagram labels (clockwise around a classroom perimeter):
- Keep this space clear
- Writable Surface for students
- Learning Process
- Clutter free windows
- Digital Display
- Calendar, Homework, etc.
- Class specific information

Take 45 seconds, once a week, to review one wall in your learning space. Does each item displayed still support learning? Did you find anything that you forgot was there? Does anything look tattered or faded? This routine can get your perimeter refreshed without creating an overwhelming amount of work.

Bonus Idea: Pick a wall and ask students to identify anything new on the wall. If they name something that has been there for months, there is a good chance that the item is just visual noise.

IDEAS TO CONSIDER

- Don't cover up windows with work. Natural light is important.
- Digitize anything that doesn't need to be referenced daily.
- Create three to four large writable spaces around the room for student collaboration.
- Use the same color palette and font around the room for a sense of unity.

IDEAS AND HABITS YOU COULD BREAK

- Thinking that a blank wall means that you do not care.
- Thinking that if students need the information, you must put it on a wall.
- Thinking that your classroom must be contained inside the physical boundaries of the space.
- Putting up borders and paper on bulletin boards. (At the very least, use one color or type.)

CLASSROOMS

The layout

The layout of a room determines how it will function, who is important, and what you care about most. In the following pages, we are going to explore how the layout can support a variety of actions.

*We are well aware that every school has differently sized and shaped classrooms, not to mention the number of students, furniture, etc. We chose a twenty-four-student class and a square format for this example.

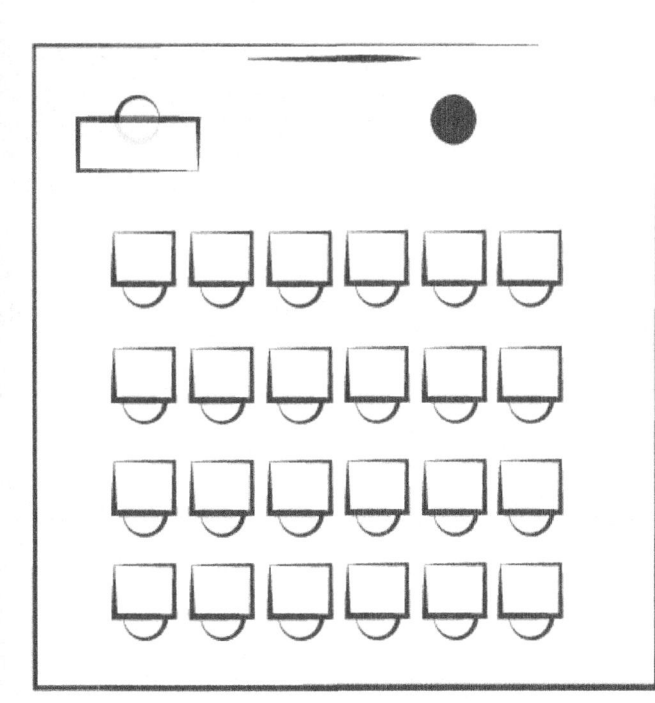

Traditional/ Teacher-centered

The work surfaces and seating all face the same direction and are the same. Teacher and student areas are clearly defined.

+ *Direct Instruction*
− *Discussions*
− *Collaboration*
− *Making*
− *Movement*

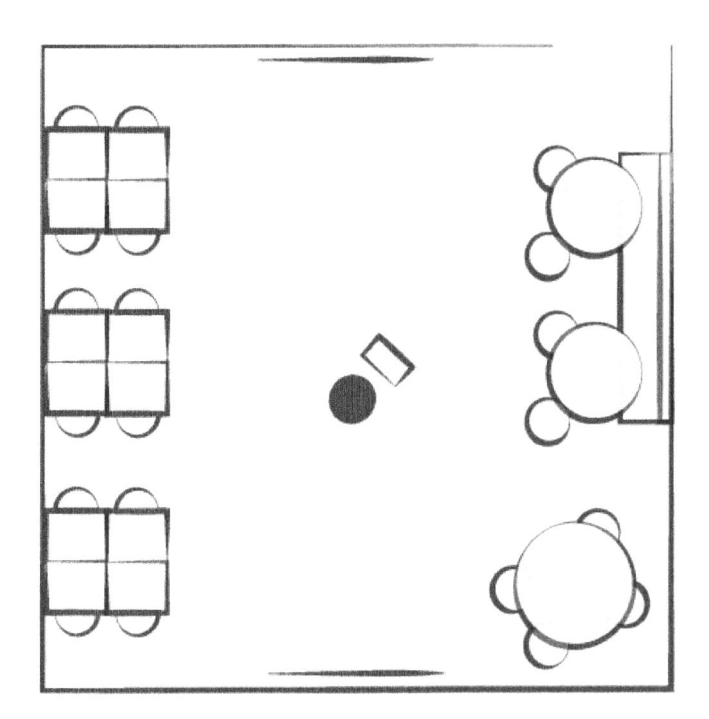

Nontraditional/ group-centered

The work surfaces and seating can easily pivot. This allows multiple focal points in the room for teaching and viewing visual displays. There is space for movement and choice of seating. Teacher and student areas are shared.

- +/− *Direct Instruction*
- + *Discussions*
- + *Collaboration*
- + *Making*
- + *Movement*

IDEAS TO CONSIDER

- Setting tables and work spaces close to the walls frees up space in the middle of the room for movement and active learning.
- Adding two digital displays allows students to see direct instruction content from anywhere in the room.
- Setting up your space to support the type of learning that you do the most. You can always re-arrange for other experiences.

IDEAS AND HABITS YOU COULD BREAK

- Believing that this has to happen at the beginning of the year.
- Thinking that you have to figure it out once and keep it that way. It should keep evolving.
- Thinking that every student should sit in the same type of seating and work on the same type of surface.

CLASSROOMS

Connect layouts to learning

The best designs sync instruction, technology tools, and space elements around the core learning verbs of a classroom Most classroom have three to five verbs that are central to the learning based grade level or subject.

What are your verbs? What do you do most? Explain, Discuss, Create? Analyze, Discover, Observe? Use the guide below to establish your verbs and help link your space to your actions.

What verbs should I choose?

Verbs should activate and accelerate learning within the classroom. What are students doing when they are at their learning best for you? Verbs should also push students to deeper thinking and deeper levels of work. Pick verbs that promote this.

How do I make them purposeful in the space?

Unpack the verbs and their purpose for students. Help them understand how activities, technology tools, and changes to the space support the core verbs. Make this an ongoing conversation topic.

How will I know when they are working?

Many students question the purpose of activities and lessons, especially as they get older. When the verbs have gotten into the DNA of your space, students will connect the verbs, activities, and *how* and *why* of its design.

ACTIONS	ACTIVITY	DESIGNS
Explain	Socratic seminar to discuss how issues of social justice have changed over time.	
Explore	Collaborative group project designed to solve an urgent community issue.	
Exhibit	Students commenting and gathering ideas from a variety of projects	

Verbs express your philosophy of active learning and help guide your design.

CLASSROOMS

Layouts explored

We gave ourselves a challenge. How can we show a variety of layouts that support different learning experiences with just traditional furniture? For each layout the number, size, and shape of desks are the same as the Traditional/Teacher-Centered Layout Style from the previous page.

Take this challenge. Think of six different ways to shape your layout to positively impact learning. Doing this stretches what you see as possible.

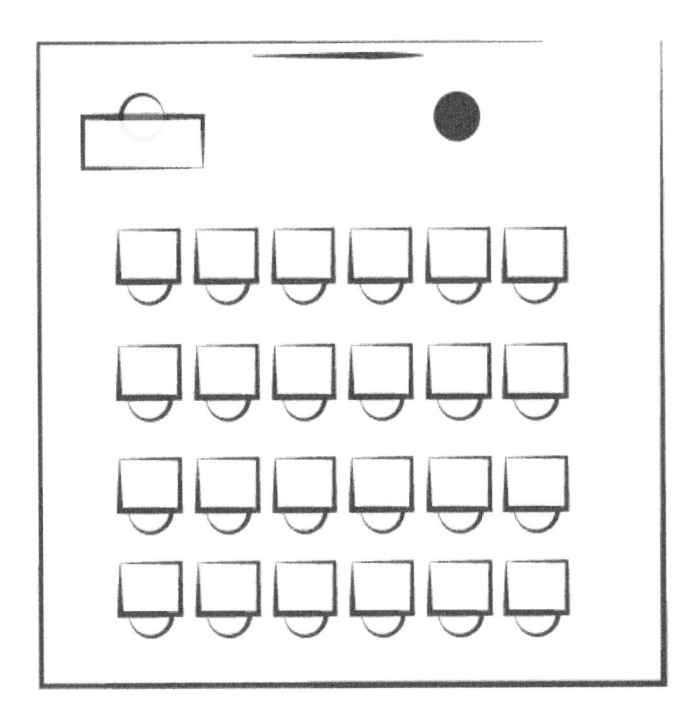

The Set-up:

1 Teacher Desk

24 Student Desks

24 Student Chairs

1 Display

Whole Group Discussion

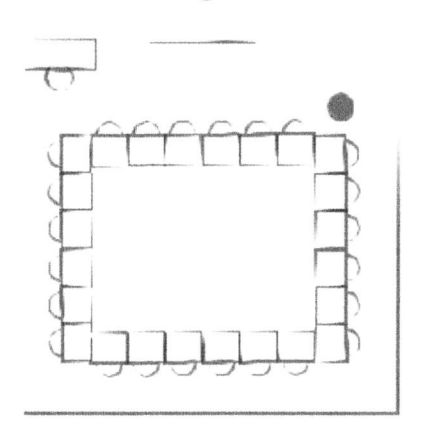

Centers

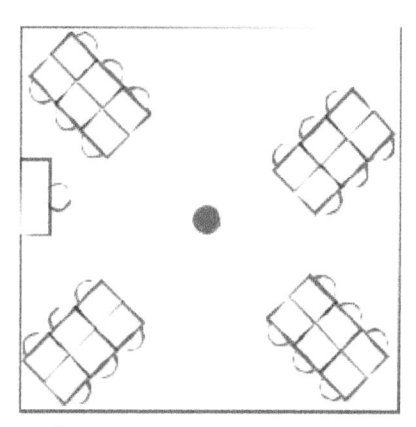

Gallery Walk

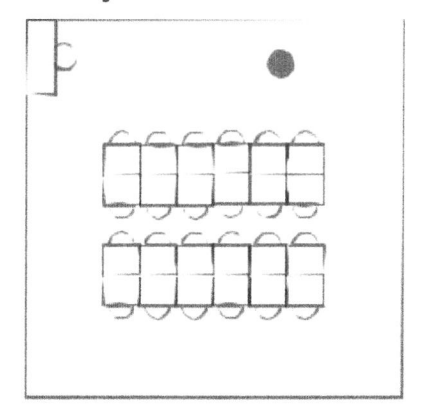

Debate

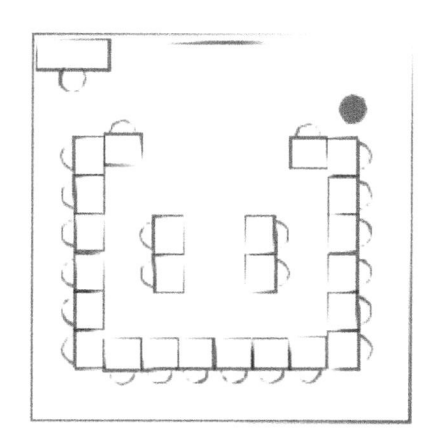

Group Work

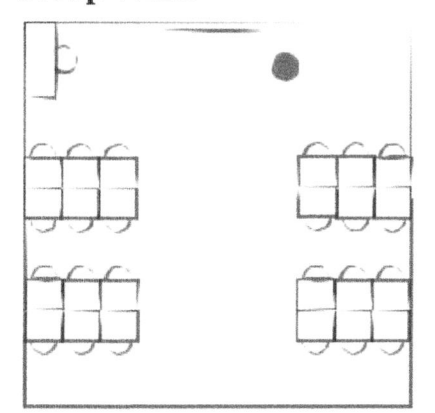

Restorative Circle

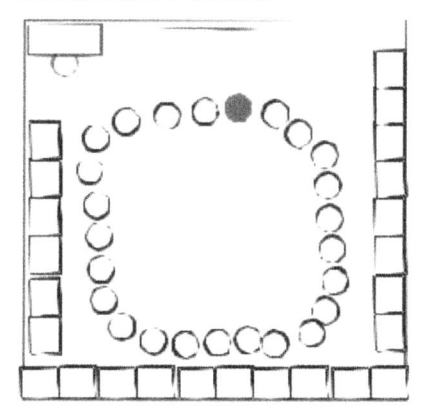

Which layout could you try?

MULTI-USE SPACES

WHAT ARE
THE OPPORTUNITIES?

Agility is the key. Many schools have spaces that get used for meetings, large gatherings, and community events. These spaces often lack a personality because they are needed for so many different things. Without design, some of these spaces lose their luster as everyday spaces for learning.

To avoid this, begin with...

- adding a physical or digital sign-up system that makes it clear that everyone has permission to use this space.
- having pictures that showcase how the space is used at its best moments.
- promoting the three to five best uses of the space (author visit, STEM challenges, interactive gallery).

Having space can be a luxury for schools, but when these larger spaces exist, we have to be intentional with their use. Too often, these spaces sit empty begging for purposeful use.

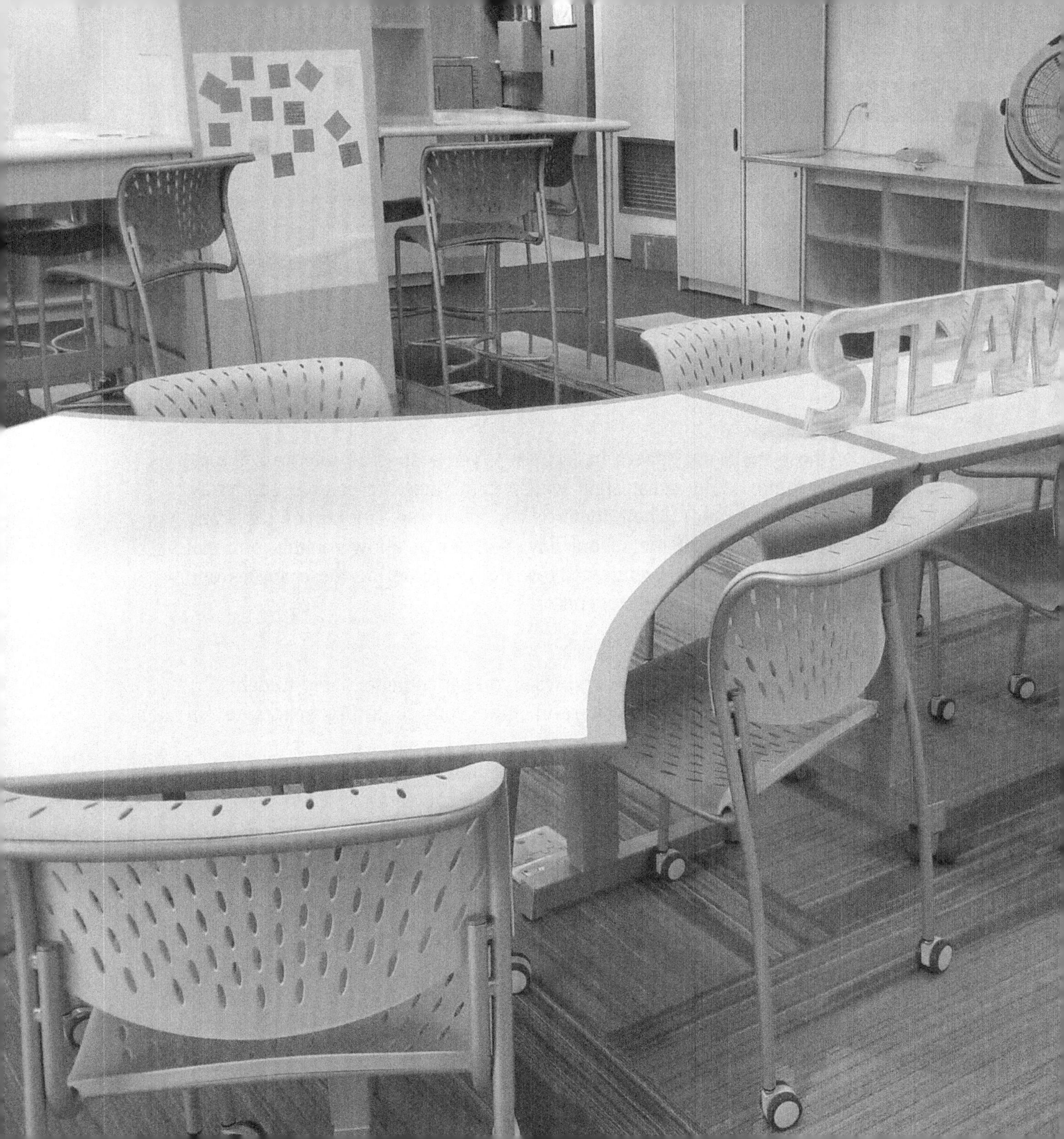

MULTI-USE SPACES

WHAT ARE THE CONSIDERATIONS?

Many of these multi-use spaces have been given a specific identity: library, conference room, lobby area, stair wells, gym, meeting rooms, cafeterias, intervention spaces, etc. Their identity can limit the amount of time and quality of use throughout the school day. We cannot allow for this minimal usage when space is at a premium. How do we re-define these spaces and introduce them to the staff and students?

First Steps: Fresh Space for New Ideas

- Assess what type of spaces you wish you had to better serve students.
- Brainstorm how might you re-imagine your multi-use spaces to fill those needs?
- Try to establish two additional uses per multi-use space.
- Test these uses with their teachers and students to see if they can effectively meets the needs.

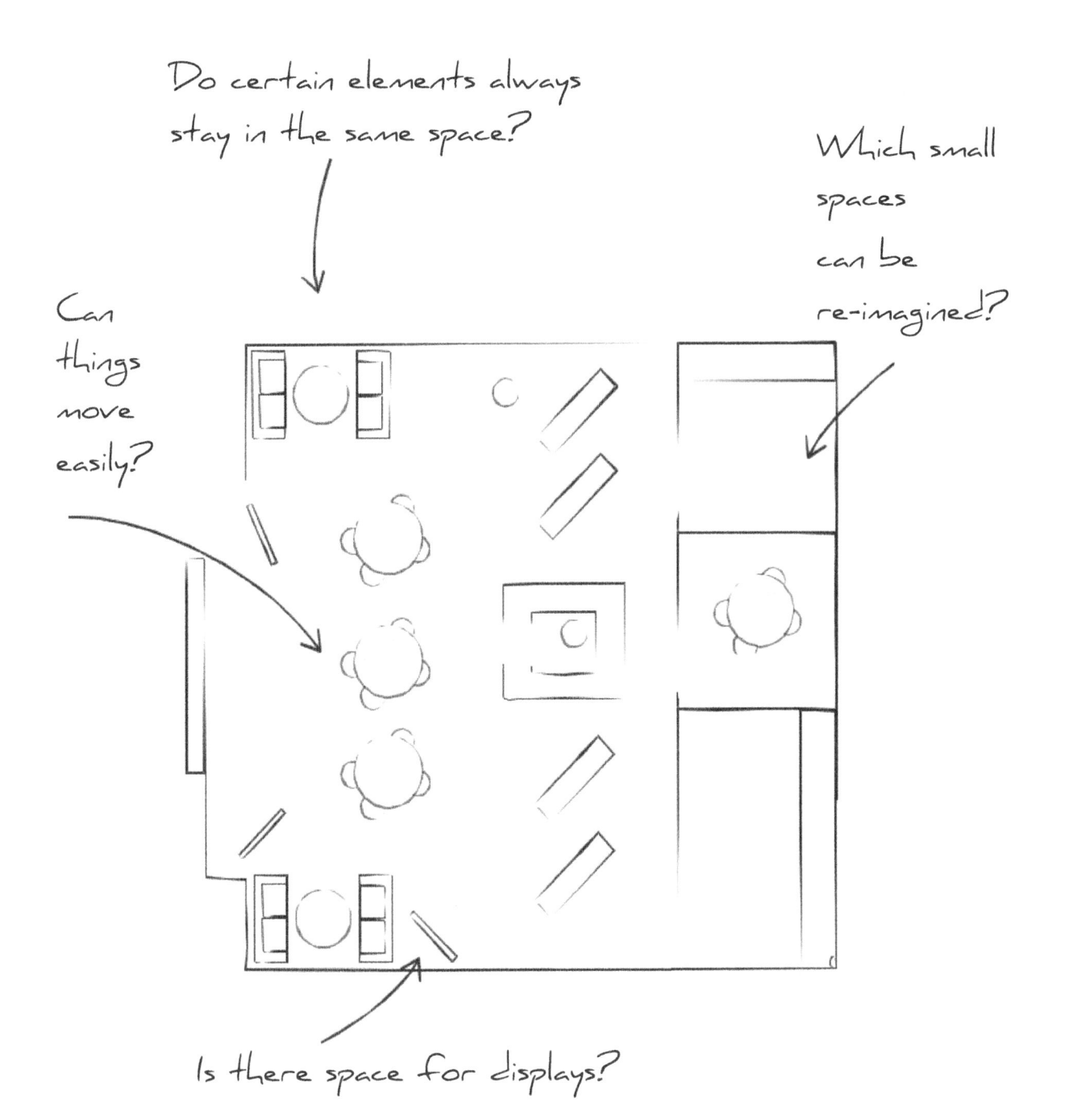

Do certain elements always stay in the same space?

Which small spaces can be re-imagined?

Can things move easily?

Is there space for displays?

MULTI-USE SPACES

Multi-use with specific purpose

The Wilson School, St. Louis, Missouri.

Rebecca has been consulting with Thad Falkner, Andrea Ruth and Melika Panneri of the Wilson School to help them re-imagine their multi-use spaces in order to support research-based instructional practices.

Why did you focus on reshaping your multi-use spaces for your project?

Wilson's mission is "to prepare students for success in an ever-changing world." In fulfilling this, we know skills of critical thinking, collaboration, creativity, communication, and character are of such importance. Putting all of them to work in a project or challenge is a strength of Wilson School. Multi-use spaces help students gain the full benefit from our instructional practices.

Where did you find success?

A success is that each space has a purpose as well as remains flexible as teachers enact activities and students approach difficult work in creative ways.

What other learning came from the project?

It was an opportunity for teachers to express their hopes for how a facility supports their work with students. Also, they told us the opportunity that exists by improving some obstacles with the layout and functions of certain spaces.

What advice would you give others working on similar things?

Do not underestimate the amount of planning that goes into designing multi-use spaces. Rebecca has amazing design skills and practical advice to make the work successful. Her work helps us fully realize and implement our vision for how instructional spaces provide even more opportunities to our students.

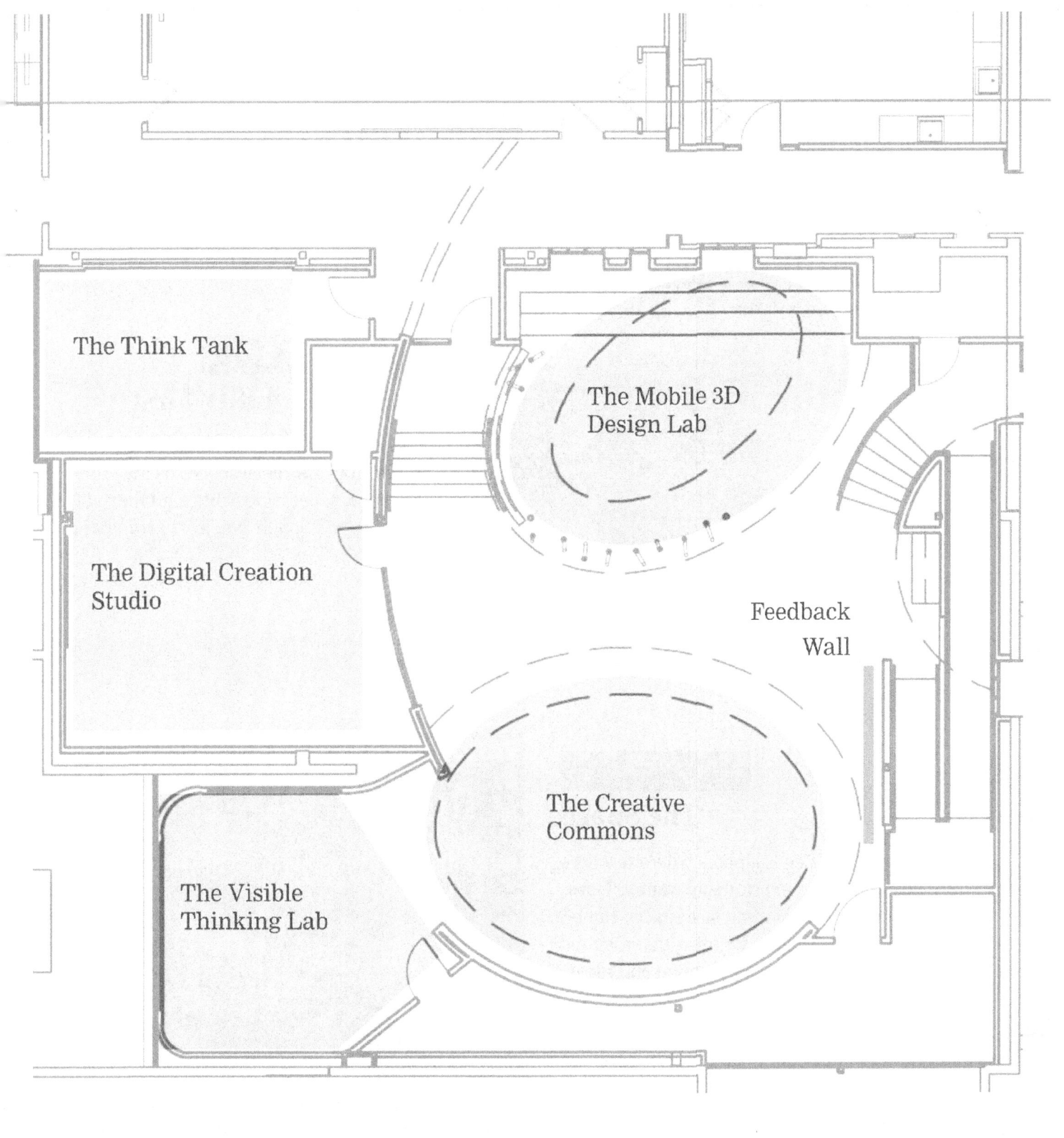

- The Think Tank
- The Digital Creation Studio
- The Mobile 3D Design Lab
- Feedback Wall
- The Creative Commons
- The Visible Thinking Lab

MULTI-USE SPACES

SPACES FOR ALL OCCASIONS

TRY IT TODAY
Think Flexibility First

Foldable, nestable, and writable tables are a great start for these spaces as they maximize what is possible, and they allow the room to convert quickly to something new.

ALSO THIS:
The Space

Every school needs a place where teachers want to work and students want to learn. Consider how your multi-use spaces can be THE space in your building that inspires innovation and ideas.

OR EVEN THIS
Host Adult Learning

When adults feel and experience the possibilities of these spaces, they are more apt to bring students into the space for similar learning. Host learning activities in these spaces.

OR MAYBE
Make it Supply-Rich

Empty spaces rarely attract a crowd. Add learning materials into these areas, so teachers and students don't have to transport as much from the classroom to use the space.

OVERLOOKED SPACES

WHAT ARE THE OPPORTUNITIES?

The smallest of spaces can scream the loudest and make an impact. Stairwells, bathrooms, teacher lounges, and many other forgotten spaces left to their own can decay and erode the other amazing work throughout the building.

Questions to ask....

- What spaces in the building undercut the mission?
- How can students help us to redesign these spaces?
- How are you keeping overlooked spaces from being forgotten?

There are so many places in the building that, when purposefully designed, can have a tremendous impact on the learning and emotional need of students and staff.

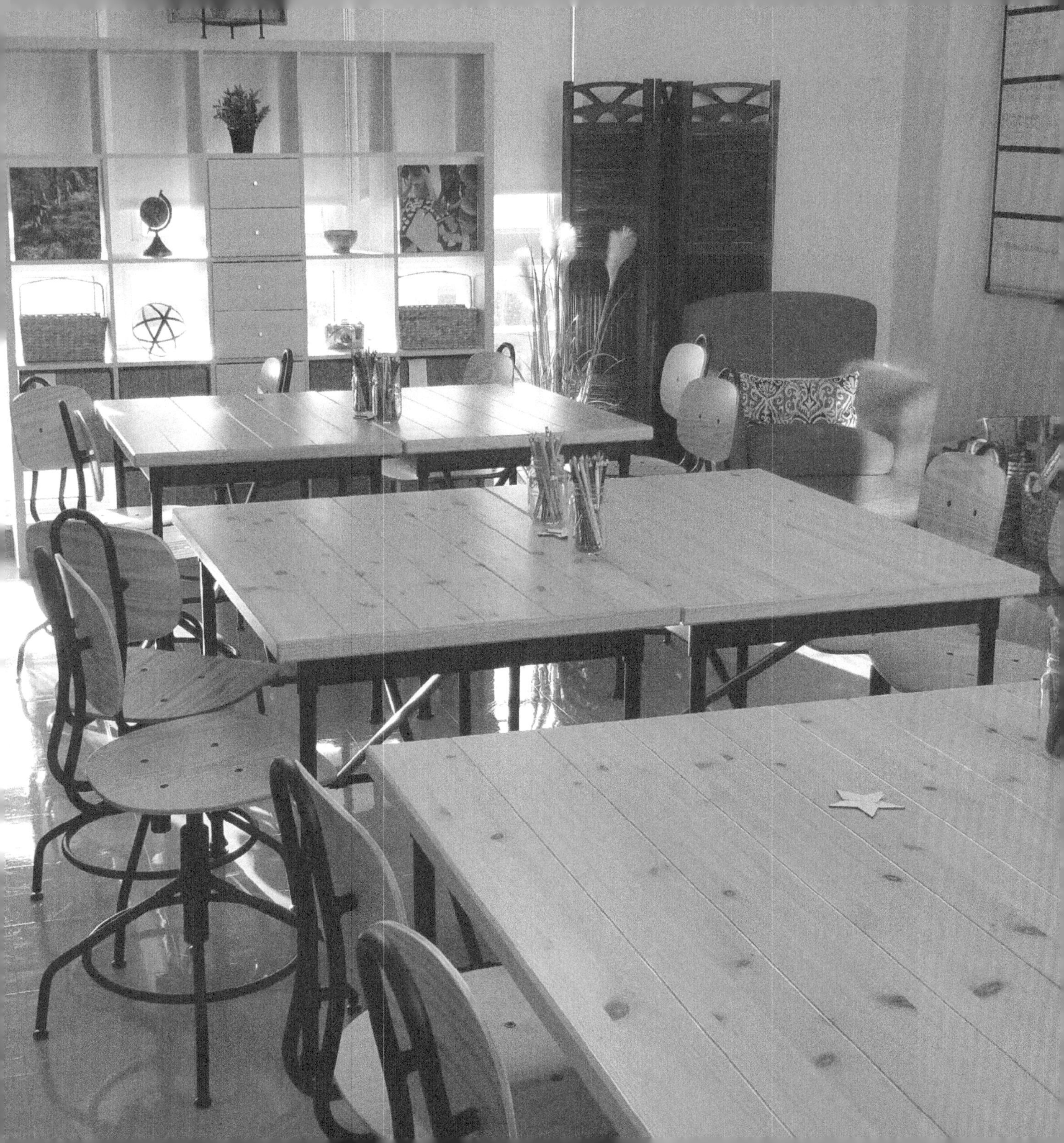

OVERLOOKED SPACES

WHAT ARE THE CONSIDERATIONS?

Small actions can allow these areas to support well being and culture. If they are allowed to steal energy from the building, they can erode other efforts. These spaces should overtly support the teachers, staff, community, and students.

First Steps: Think Small
- What can you remove? These spaces are often default storage areas filled with boxes and furniture.
- What can you add? A few small touches can make a space more welcoming and give it purpose.
- Paint and lighting can be life-giving for these spaces.

Reality Check: Empty spaces that are "being prototyped" are better than tired, worn, cluttered spaces.

Are these respectful to all humans? ↓

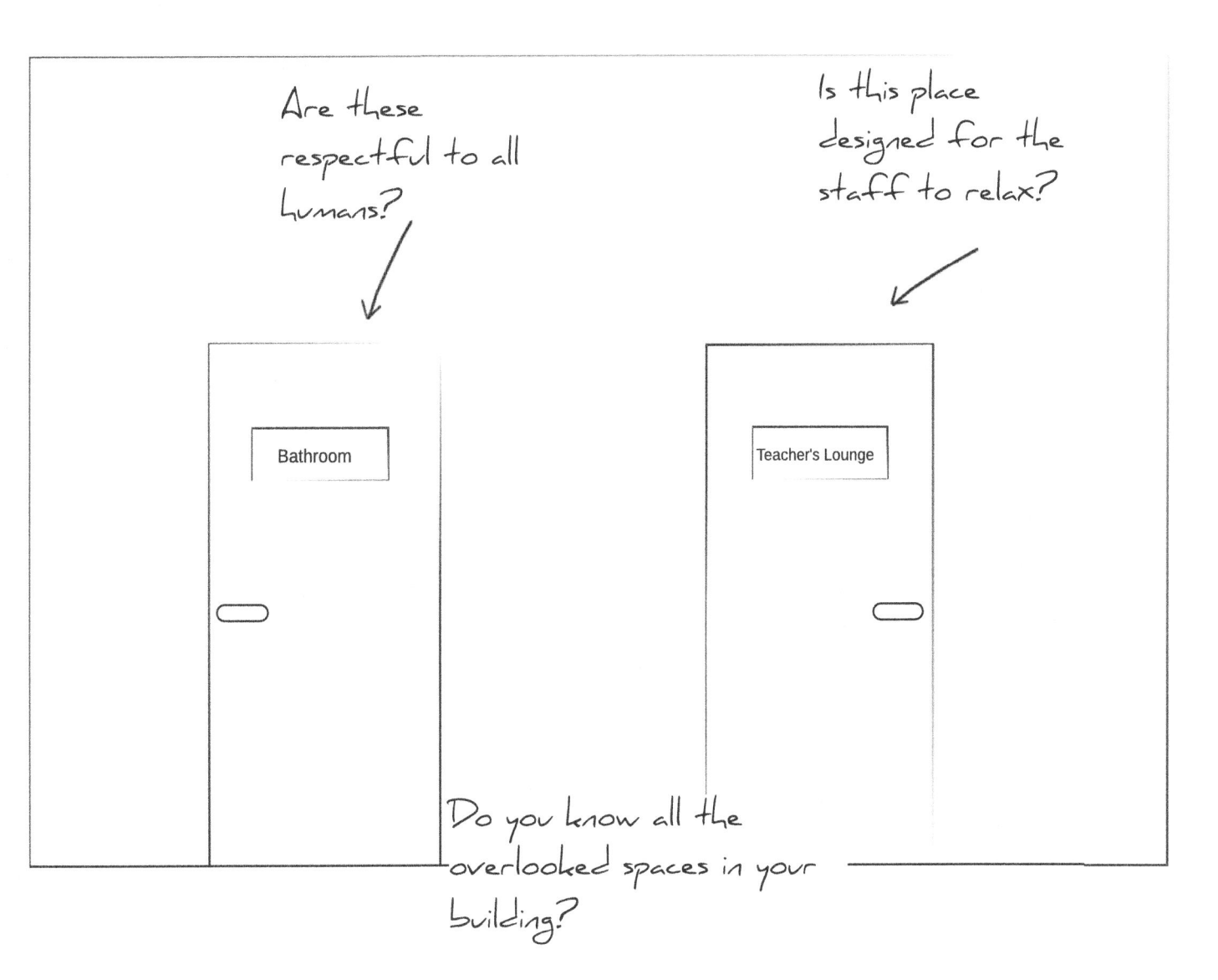

Bathroom

Is this place designed for the staff to relax? ↙

Teacher's Lounge

Do you know all the overlooked spaces in your building?

OVERLOOKED SPACES

Space Designed for Professionals

Dr. Trent Daniel, Lake Brantley High School, Florida

Why did you focus on reshaping the staff-room for your project?

One of the main priorities for the campus was facility improvement. The district funded a major renovation of a brand-new beautifully modernized building; however, the older part of the campus also needed attention especially the faculty work rooms. The faculty work rooms were not conducive to collaborative interaction. The setup was dated and didn't match our expectation of Professional Learning Communities.

Where did you find success?

We coordinated the same styles and patterns with the new building. This provided a more cohesive "look" for the campus. My team and I also created different spaces for the different work rooms, so each department would have an "identity" by color. This also helped to give each department ownership to their new areas as all of the faculty was reorganized from a grade level set up to a department configuration.

What advice would you give others working on similar things?

Try to be open-minded, include the faculty/staff, and listen to other's opinions as much as possible. One area that I believe we did well is sending teachers to see different types of modern student furniture (flexible seating) for the classroom. We visited three different schools, and then we selected furniture for the new building.

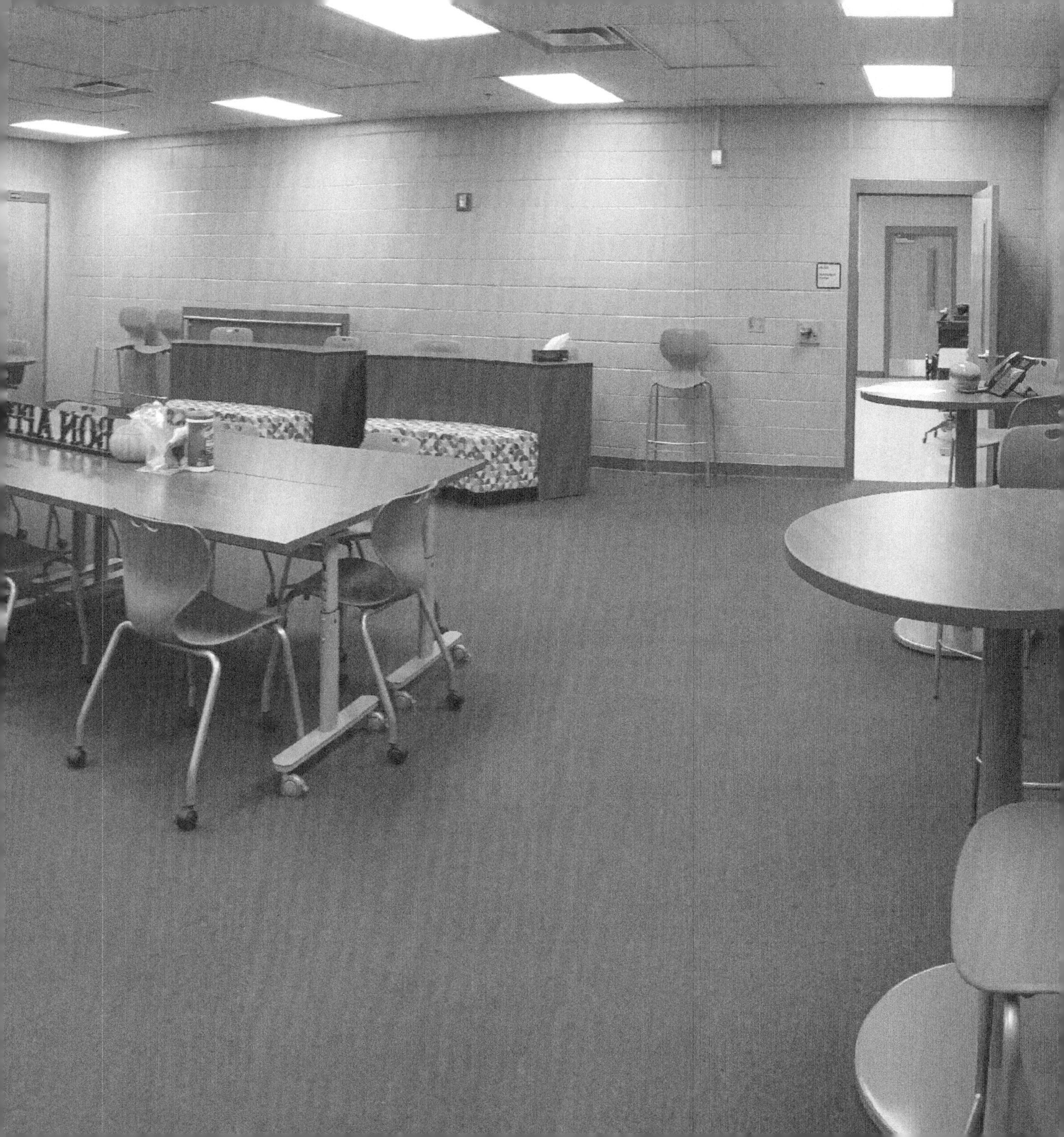

OVERLOOKED SPACES

DON'T FORGET ABOUT US

According to research from New Zealand and Australian academics, published in the Asia-Pacific Journal of Teacher Education, a staffroom not only functions as a physical space, but also a social, cultural and emotional space for its occupants (Hunter, Rossi, Tinning, Flanagan & Macdonald, 2011).

TRY IT TODAY

Choose a Purpose

Spaces for teachers to gather can't be everything, or they will become nothing and collect junk. Send a message to the staff that they are valued through the spaces that you design for them to work and relax.

ALSO THIS:

Paint and Personalize

Make sure that the bathrooms tell the story that students are cared for in every space. Find ways spruce up the bathrooms with paint and personal touches.

OR EVEN THIS
Behind Every Door

We have a tendency to forget the things behind locked doors, but we need to make sure that all spaces support your culture and mission. Well-designed schools have no junk drawers.

OR MAYBE
Empty the Closet

Storage in all schools is at premium, and in many overlooked spaces, we are storing unneeded and dated things. Purge these spaces, and hold space for a new strategy for storage.

This journey to see the entire building as purposeful space for learning will transform how you and others serve students.

WELCOME SPACES

THE OUTSIDE OF SCHOOL

HALLWAYS

Classroom redesign is essential, but the power of this work comes through a comprehensive rethink of all spaces to positively impact culture and learning.

LIBRARIES AND MULTI-USE SPACES

What other spaces could add to the intentional design of the school?

CLASSROOMS

OVERLOOKED SPACES

Some Final Design Tools

The design of schools is never a standard process, but there are some common elements that arise for most design teams. This section provides insights and resources to support the design journey and the learning that follows.

- WHY LEADERS CONSIDER SPACE
- IMPACT OF SPACES
- HOW SPACE AFFECTS CULTURE
- PURPOSEFUL DESIGN
- LEARNING SPACE MINDSETS

Omission is a form of design. Schools not in design conversations are designing with their silence.

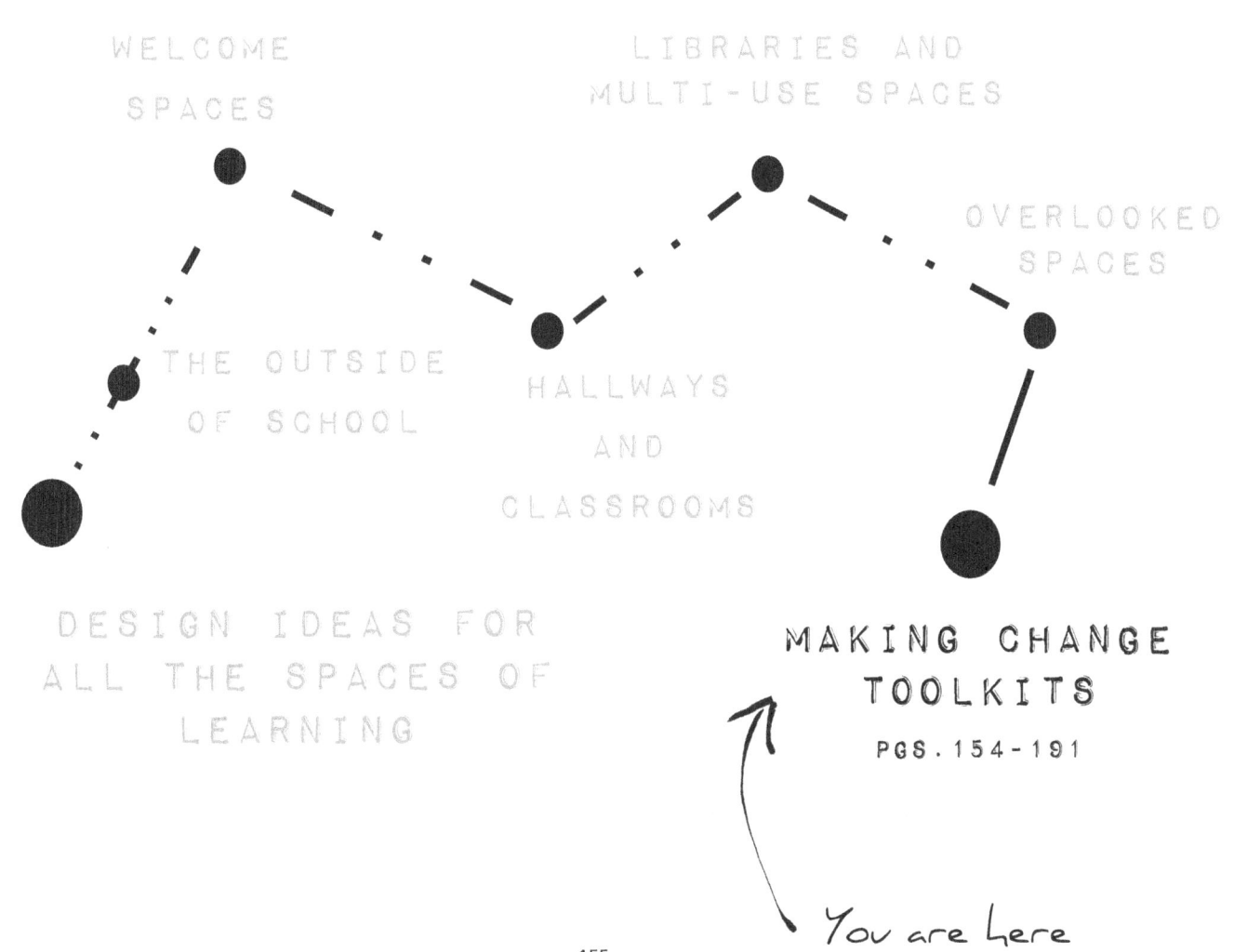

WELCOME SPACES

LIBRARIES AND MULTI-USE SPACES

THE OUTSIDE OF SCHOOL

HALLWAYS AND CLASSROOMS

OVERLOOKED SPACES

DESIGN IDEAS FOR ALL THE SPACES OF LEARNING

MAKING CHANGE TOOLKITS
PGS. 154-191

You are here

CLASSROOM MANAGEMENT

Supporting and Managing

How can we support and manage self-regulation in a flexible learning environment?

This question comes up a lot. After the spaces are designed and the excitement has worn off, teachers and students may find it difficult to adjust to a new environment in which the old expectations and rules don't fit with the new mindset. Teachers complain of distracting behavior, too many choices, and students having trouble with self-control. This is all normal. We have some tips to help everyone navigate this change and develop autonomy and agency for learners.

But first, some wise words:

"I found that thinking about behavior objectively, as a skill to be taught rather than simply as good or bad, was immensely helpful in my ability to guide children in learning to control their behavior. Some children enter school without the self-regulation skills necessary for school success. We must meet these children where they are and teach them the skills they need to be successful in the classroom."

How to Teach Self-Regulation - Parrish 2018

*"...autonomy and agency are embedded in and accomplished through the interaction between the **opportunities a student has to participate and the ways they take up these opportunities**. It encompasses a **student's capacity to monitor and guide his or her own learning progress and participation** using the resources (people, ideas, things) in the setting"*

Fostering Student Learning Agency and Autonomy- Cowie - Moreland & Otrel-Cass 2013

Developing Autonomy and Agency Work

● CHOICES FOR LEARNING
What can you let them choose? Seating? Location? What they create? How they engage in the learning?

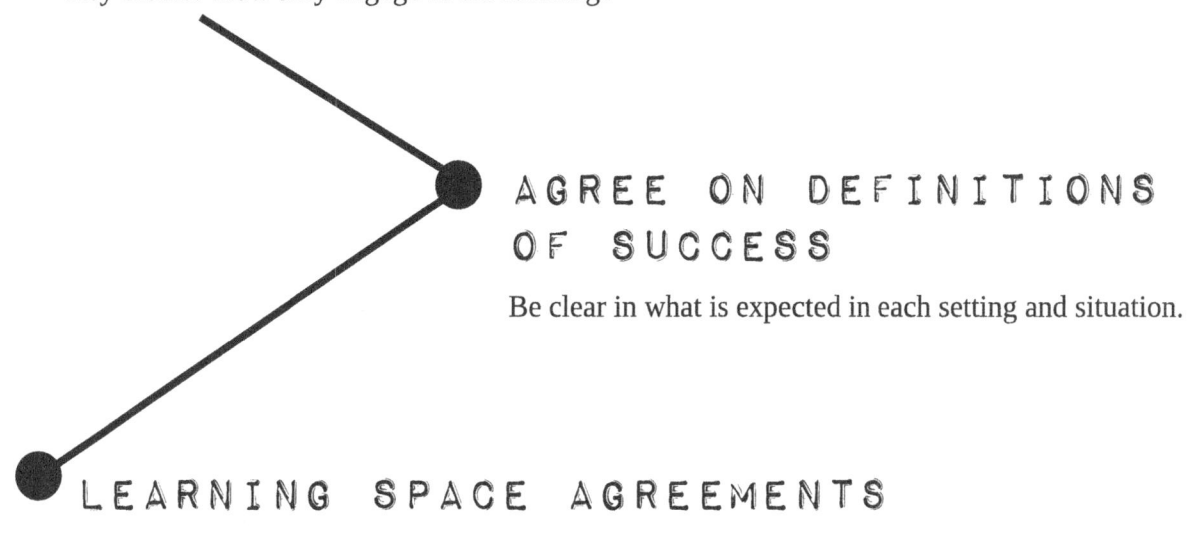

AGREE ON DEFINITIONS OF SUCCESS
Be clear in what is expected in each setting and situation.

LEARNING SPACE AGREEMENTS
Create something that is visible in the space, agreed on by everyone, and referred to often.

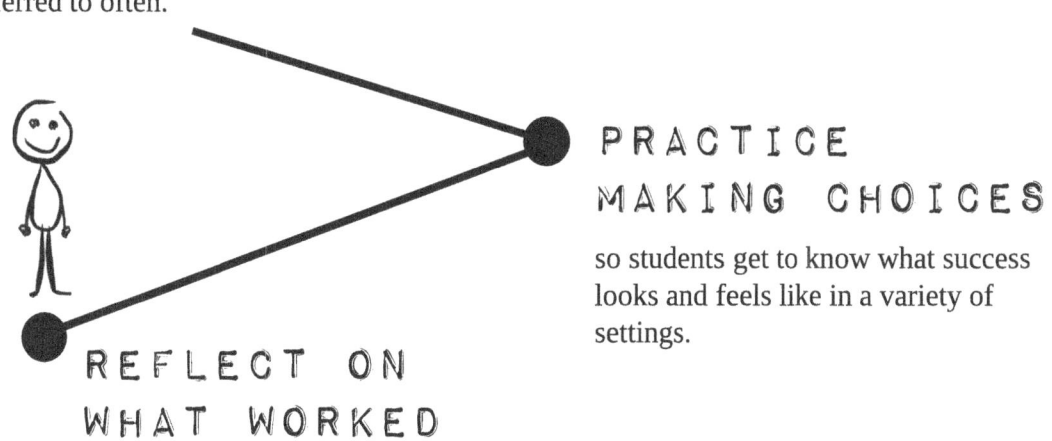

PRACTICE MAKING CHOICES
so students get to know what success looks and feels like in a variety of settings.

REFLECT ON WHAT WORKED
so students know what to choose next time.

CLASSROOM MANAGEMENT

In an ideal learning environment...

How many choices should we give?

We know that this process can feel overwhelming, you want to give your students an ideal learning environment that supports their agency and autonomy, yet it feels chaotic at times and not conducive to learning. Use these steps to help craft a plan around managing your flexible, agile learning environment.

CHOICES FOR LEARNING

We often start with too many choices. It does not have to be a "all or nothing." Maybe the appropriate number of choices is two or three. Those choices can vary depending on the activity and the student's age. At times, there may be no choices given.

In a study, researchers found that by offering two books, students read longer and were more satisfied with their choice than when more options were given.

"... offering children too many choices makes them less likely to engage with their final selection."

<u>Are You Offering Your Children Too Many Choices?</u>- *Maimaran 2017*

Start small and don't overwhelm your students with choices. You can always add more later.

DEFINE SUCCESS

When students know what is appropriate in each type of learning (whole group engagement and choice seating time), they are set up for success, so start with a good definition of what is expected in each situation.

- Good definitions help us create a common language from which we can create a common set of expectations.
- Good definitions are valuable assets. They allow us to assess situations better, have more meaningful conversations and make better decisions. In contrast, imprecise definitions make it difficult to even agree on what we are talking about. The conversations end up circling around, going nowhere.
- **Good definitions are precise and understood by everyone who uses them.**

You can do this work with your students. It gives them more agency and helps them understand the "why" behind the words.

Example Definitions...

Whole Group Engagement

In whole group engagement, we are facing the person talking, and our bodies and voices are quiet. We are actively listening and developing questions about the material being presented.

Choice Seating

In choice seating, we make our choices quickly. We have our materials, and we are focused on our work or learning, not distracting to other learners.

The Ritual of Choice

Three things to help the group and each student make choices. Start with a positive environment.

- **Give two:** The chair, or the floor. The sofa, or the stool.
- **Limit the time:** Is 20 seconds enough? Do you want them to choose ahead of time?
- **Be Consistent:** Offer choice for certain activities and not for others. Avoid confusion.

Also, research shows that giving kids a say:

- *builds respect,*
- *strengthens community,*
- *invites cooperation,*
- *develops problem-solving skills, and capitalizes on kids' normal human need for power and control.*

<u>Five Guidelines for Giving Kids Choices</u>- *Leyba 2016.*

CLASSROOM MANAGEMENT

In an ideal learning environment we...

Create norms, practice and reflect.

This is a practice to develop self-directed and reflective learners, but without some scaffolding, these new choices can feel overwhelming and like a trap for kids who don't have a lot of practice making good choices.

LEARNING SPACE AGREEMENTS

- Choose a format that it is most appropriate for your class (checklist, contract, co-created norms)
- Have different expectations for group collaboration, direct instruction, and choice seating times
- Include students in the creation of these agreements; otherwise, they are just rules.

PRACTICE

- Explain: We are going to do "_____" which should look, feel and sound like...
- Remind students, What is your job right now? Which supplies do you need?

REFLECT

- Ask your students: How did that experience/space feel? What could you do differently next time? What is the kind thing to do now? (or from now on)

A place to begin...

As we move to greater student choice in our learning spaces, we will always hit road bumps despite the best norms and agreements. Here is a strategy that works in a variety of situations.

Priming Self-Regulation

This strategy helps students practice and reinforce desirable work habits and build awareness of what is appropriate in each situation. Here is how it works: as students settle into their chosen environment do a quick "checklist" about what they need: *"Do you have all the materials (be specific) that you need? Are you away from distractions? Did you choose a space that supports this type of learning?"*

Then, do a "check-in" that asks them to focus on their senses or "how" the space should feel: *"We are doing silent reading for the next 20 minutes. Let's take a few moments to listen to how that should sound. Now, you should be comfortable. Check-in with your body on how it feels. Is it quiet and restful and ready to read?"*

Repeat this as often as necessary so that students always know what is expected.

More Support

Some students will need more time and extra support. Here are some options:

- **Self-Monitoring**
  Print it out and have them keep it with their things.
- **Non-Verbal Cues**
  Have the student choose the cue. Practice and check in often.
- **Plan Ahead**
  Before a choice moment, have students make a plan of where they will sit, and how they will work, self-evaluate, and reflect.

Crafting the story of a space is what allows everyone to see the possibilities.

COMMUNICATION PLAN

HOW ARE YOU SCULPTING A NEW NARRATIVE?

Hearts and Minds

Changing learning spaces without changing hearts and minds about the realities of today's student learning experience can leave audiences guessing about the motives and meaning of shifts in space design.

It's About Learning

Any communication strategy must showcase how the space design changes are components of the district strategic initiatives and connects to the vision and mission.

Keep the focus on how spaces affect learning to avoid the perception that the changes are an interior decorating exercise.

In our noisy information age, we must repeat our message often in various media.

`COMMUNICATIONS PLAN`

Showcasing Learning Spaces...

The communication design can be as important as the space design.

Identifying audiences

Schools should identify all potential audiences, both internally and externally, that need targeted messaging around this work. Create a detailed plan around both message and media for each audience.

Audiences include: teachers, secretaries, counselors, custodians, maintenance staff, students, leadership, parents, tax payers, business owners, civic leaders, and partner organizations.

SCHOOLS NEED TO MAKE SURE THAT THEIR MESSAGE DOESN'T GET LOST IN THE NOISE OF LIFE.

The science of marketing

To do this, it is important to consider all of the media options that are available. Many audiences receive their communication from one or two channels and fully mute the others. If we are speaking into the wrong channels, valuable resources are lost. It's as though we are yelling into the forest.

Focus the message

The messaging needs to be coherent and simple. Make sure that internal audiences know that the design work will support students in both their academic and social-emotional growth. The audience beyond the walls of the school needs to know that where kids learn matters, and the demands of society are asking us to reshape and rethink all aspects of school.

Student and Teacher Voice

Bring students and teachers into the communications strategy. Let them be lead voices to build energy around this work. Our students know the power of learning spaces. They know that it brings them joy and raises their interest in schools, and this story is essential for all to hear.

KEEP YOUR LANGUAGE FOCUSED ON LEARNING.

WHAT DO YOU SAY?

Learning-Focused
- "Here are some of the ways students create."
- "Here is one way we personalize learning."
- "This room allows students more autonomy and independence."

Stuff-focused
- "We have a 3D printer!"
- "We are 1:1!"
- "We just got new furniture."

COMMUNICATIONS PLAN

"These are the artifacts students have created demonstrate our core values."

"This is our process for solving problems."

"These artifacts allow students to share and reflect on their growth."

HOW DO YOU SHOW?

"These are our professionally-designed posters that teach our core values."

"Here are a bunch of projects."

"This is where we post our test results."

LEARNING FROM ANYWHERE

Learning is happening beyond the typical classroom space more than ever. We are clearly no longer bound to the building.

The user experience of school is rapidly shifting. Online and virtual learning are being layered into physical space learning to create a variety of hybrid models. This requires educators to design multiple spaces into one coherent user experience (UX) for students.

Teachers are now UX designers that facilitate learning across spaces. This requires enhanced mindsets that help to craft a fluid journey for all students.

As designers, how can we craft easy access to information? How can we communicate in clear ways without instant feedback from students? How can we model best practices around time and space so that students can take these concepts into their home learning environments? Can we build coherency between digital and physical spaces while maintaining the same school culture?

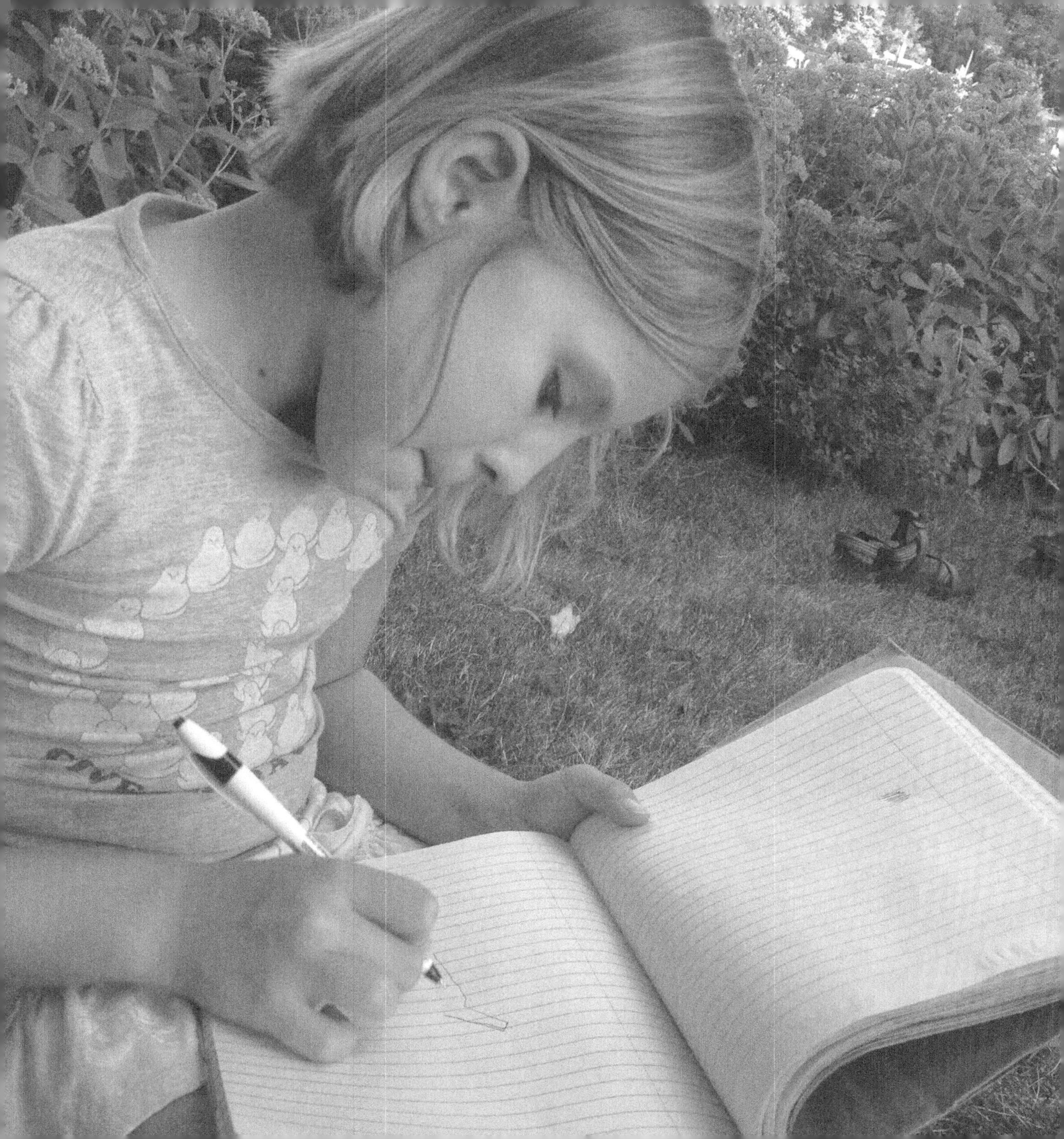

LEARNING FROM ANYWHERE

Mindsets for Virtual Personalized Learning Design

Think about the design mindsets through this lens.

Rebecca worked with San Francisco based educators and leaders: Zareen Poonen Levien, Benjamin Klaus and E'leva Hughes Gibson to re-define the Design Mindsets in order to support teachers with their virtual learning environments.

Addition by Subtraction

1. **Select and use a few digital tools that fulfill multiple purposes and learning opportunities**
   - **Why?** Using fewer tools allows students to focus most of their energy on the content/skills learning instead of how to learn new tools. This also lowers student and family anxiety and helps them feel successful.
   - **How?** Look for tools that display content with clarity. Find digital tools that allow for an easy work flow for students. Some of the best tools provide creation tools and support for students in one place.

2. **Create a simple schedule / checklist for students to follow each day/week**
   - **Why?** Clear, predictable schedules help students and families know what to expect and how to manage their time. This will also help them keep track and complete assignments.
   - **How?** Provide a checklist. Group assignments by day. Choose a method, keep it simple, and be consistent.

3. **Keep your learning platform focused on current learning.**
   - **Why?** Online platforms can quickly become cluttered and confusing. Clear out old assignments to help students find current assignments more easily and quickly.
   - **How?** Each week move assignments to a "Previous Assignments" category and archive older activities in your digital learning space.

Equity and Agency

1. **Build independent learners by teaching the unique learning routines, skills and tools in the digital space.**
   - **Why?** Students can build confidence by becoming self-sufficient with tools and a predictable structures. This frees up synchronous time with teachers to maximize time spent on feedback and content-related conversations.
   - **How?** Explicitly teach learning routines, skills and tools in the beginning (reinforce with video tutorials so families always have access), and continue to repeat the same structures so that students can just focus on content and skills and build independence.

2. **Provide weekly feedback opportunities through your digital space to support families' success. Support all families as teaching and learning partners.**
   - **Why?** We aim to validate the diverse needs of our families and continuously adjust our support so that we cultivate self-efficacy beliefs and positive academic mindsets in our families and students.
   - **How?** With students: The goal is to have consistent, clear, validating feedback for learning. Frequent opportunities for student-to-teacher feedback. With families: The goal is to do a weekly check-in that clarifies learning goals, invites questions and insights into families needs (Feedback form or questions weekly for students and families).

3. **Create digital learning experiences designed to support each and every student. Empower all learners with choice with space and time.**
   - **Why?** Build student engagement, ownership of their learning and meta-cognitive skills by cultivating the mindset of how to approach learning objectives. So that they are empowered to drive their learning, share their discoveries through a reflective process that highlights their unique lenses on the world, skills and identities.
   - **How?** Provide one choice per learning experience for learners (example of expression and example of engagement) // (tech and non-tech option)

LEARNING FROM ANYWHERE

Push vs. Pull

1. **Leverage synchronous time for pull: connecting, collaborating, and fostering greater understanding of the material.**
   - **Why?** When we are together we can use the time for getting to know students, interacting and building SEL skills, collaborating, asking questions, assessing understanding and building excitement.
   - **How?** Leverage synchronous time to confer and interact with students to monitor new student learning and build on their thinking.

2. **Leverage asynchronous time for push: new content, reflection and feedback.**
   - **Why?** Empower students with self-paced learning structures. By sharing new content asynchronously, we let students choose the space and time that is best for them and their families' needs.
   - **How?** By pre-recording learning videos and developing or choosing content that is self-paced and responsive to student learning needs. Give students opportunities to record and share their thinking asynchronously through tools like Seesaw.

3. **Design learning experiences that pull from student interests and lived experiences.**
   - **Why?** Emotion and cognition are interdependent processes. It is literally impossible to build memories, engage in complex thoughts or make meaningful decisions without emotion. *Why Emotions Are Integral to Learning-Immordino-Yang 2016*
   - **How?** Start by discovering your students interests and preferences: build relationships, find out what sparks their curiosity, uncover their prior-knowledge. Engage students to see content as meaningful to their lives. Support students in choosing unique ways to showcase their discoveries with an authentic audience.

Process over Product

1. **Educator:** Show the learning/experience journey in your digital space; where to begin, what to do next, how to be successful.
   - **Why?** When students and families know what to expect, they can focus on the content, skill development and deeper learning. Students develop agency, a sense of purpose and time management to complete their work successfully.
   - **How?** A simple, predictable visual that shows what is expected. Include steps and examples (variety is ideal) so that every student feels confident about their path.

2. **Learner:** Record reflections throughout the learning experience using the available digital tools in the space.
   - **Why?** Through consistent reflection opportunities, students will develop self-awareness and metacognitive skills and learn to make their thinking visible. This serves as both a documentation of growth and important informal feedback on instruction for educators.
   - **How?** Build reflective questions into the process of learning in a predictable routine (e.g. end of every day or at specific points during the week).

3. **Collective:** Use digital tools to share and reflect on in-progress work. It will make thinking visible and gather peer feedback.
   - **Why?** Feedback requires that we pause and think about our progress. It empowers students by focusing more on the learning community (peers) and less on authority (teacher). Students build critical thinking skills in analyzing others' work.
   - **How?** Feedback is most effective when it is constructive, specific, timely and frequent. Model giving feedback on student work during synchronous time. Provide language protocols for productive feedback and build feedback steps into the process for all content areas. Create opportunities for students to share their ideas with others.

LEARNING FROM ANYWHERE

Our homes are now serving as spaces for teaching and learning to a greater degree than ever before. Consider these design tips and ideas.

Teaching Tips for Home

Change up your "desk":

Designate three spaces that support different postures (like your kitchen bar, sofa, dining table, or coffee table) to get your body moving. Try to stay no more than three hours in each space. You can even connect each space to a task that works best in that location.

Get close to green:

Strategically place plants near your work areas to brighten your day! Biophilic design reconnects people to nature and brings green spaces inside. It is widely believed that plants can reduce stress, help with focus, increase immunity and also help productivity.

Include rituals:

Try to set up a few simple rituals that relax and energize you and help you pass your day. Rituals have been shown to reduce anxiety and improve performance. Set up rituals that define your day, like a celebratory chocolate after work or an early morning weekday video chat with your best friend.

Visualize your progress:

Make an accomplishment list each day or week in which you get to check off each item. Make this list only for non-work-related items, like taking a shower, reading a book, exercising, and treating yourself to a dessert. Tracking progress helps us increase our happiness, which is optimal for creativity.

Create some physical white space:

We do some of our best thinking off-screen. A large piece of paper (or a few pages taped together) or a journal can be a great backdrop for brainstorming, planning, or a place for virtual meeting doodles. Writing by hand helps us detach from our screens and gives our minds new outlets for expression.

Supporting Students Learning at Home

Learning continues beyond the bell, and these ideas and tips can help students learn no matter where they are located.

Check the lighting

This may be something that you can't control, but the lighting that works for your home office might not be right for student learning. Ask your child if they have enough natural light or which lights in the house are best for their learning. These little details can make learning easier and more enjoyable.

Space and time are very hard to separate

Create vessels of time for getting things completed, but make them a bit larger than needed and allow for some flexibility. A tight schedule that dictates exactly when things happen doesn't rely on learning science. Our students need brain breaks, the freedom to swap items around in the schedule, and some free range learning time.

The right noise matters

Talk to your child about what learning they can do with and without noise. Support your child with the noise that they need. When can they listen to music and work? When do they need real quiet? Don't forget to ask what in the house is distracting. Sometimes absolute quiet is the worst distraction.

Learning is experienced based

This is a great time to create experiences. Play games. Laugh together. Watch a movie. Listen to great music. Tell a story. Go for a walk. Teachers know that these moments matter in their classrooms as well. Create space for experiences.

The right supplies to learn

Students shouldn't have to wander all around the house to find what they need. Discuss with your child what supplies are needed, and how can you get them as close to the learning as possible.

You have insider information as a teacher on how to set the stage for great learning. Share that with parents and lead them in the small ways they can support their students. What may feel obvious to you might not be obvious to parents.

MEASURING SUCCESS

Finding new ways to claim success...

When school and district leaders and design teams embark on redesigning their learning spaces, they should set metrics to help determine whether or not their projects are successful.

When redesigning your learning environments, don't settle for metrics that aren't in line with your mission.

Use the strategies on the following pages to choose the actions that will positively impact the metrics that matter for these projects.

LEARNING SPACES ARE IMPACTFUL WHEN THEY...

LOWER
- ANXIETY
- STRESS
- TEACHER BURNOUT

RAISE
- ENGAGEMENT
- JOY
- POSITIVE LEARNING ENERGY

ENHANCE
- NATURAL LIGHT
- ACOUSTICS
- AIR QUALITY

CULTIVATING SUCCESS

Space alone doesn't bring success. It is the actions inside those spaces that bring true progress. Here are some strategies.

Joy and Engagement

Classroom joy and engagement aren't the same for every student. They can be personal to the learner, so some of these ideas will work for some and other ideas will support other students.

- **Create Feedback Loops-** Ask students how different areas of the building impact their learning. Use this feedback to make changes.
- **Moments of Gratitude-** Have students talk about someone or something in the classroom that has been supportive of them as a student.
- **Positive Energy-** Smiles and laughter are keys to a joyful space. Be intentional about increasing both.
- **Recognize and Praise Engagement in Different Forms-** Identify high engagement in all forms and call it out.

Lowering Stress and Anxiety

Spaces where we don't feel successful can cause us stress and anxiety. Classrooms for many students can be a perpetual space of struggle. It is also worth noting that anxious and over-stressed bodies produce diminishing academic returns.

- **Model Failing Forward-** As teachers, we make mistakes everyday, and our ability to be vulnerable with these mistakes in front of students can relieve some stress.
- **Design Moments of Success-** As you support students in growing a pattern of academic success, start with easy wins for students.
- **Name your Emotions-** Students have trouble naming the physiological things happening to their bodies when they are filled with stress and anxiety. They need to know that they are OK and that there are ways to reduce the impact of the stress and anxiety that will come through life.

MEASURING SUCCESS

The Well-Being of Teachers

Well teachers are the only options for crafting well classrooms. If you want to measure the well-being of students, get tuned into the wellness of teachers.

- **Create Permissions**- Design systems for teachers to easily take time to support their children at home. Extra paperwork, pressure, and unwritten rules can lead to unneeded stress in this area.
- **Use Professional Decision-Making Strategies**- Let teachers know that you trust their decisions, and you want them to make real-time decisions to meet kids' needs.
- **Design to Support Well Being**- This co-created space would allow quiet, relaxation, and moments to escape from the stress of the day.

Natural Light, Air Quality, and Acoustics

Though some of these fall beyond the control of many individual keepers of space, it is important to know a few ways to recapture that control when possible.

- **Open the Mini-Blinds**- Don't sacrifice security, but allow as much light into the room as possible.
- **Tilt the Talk**- If there is a place in the room that creates an echo or makes it hard to hear for students, consider tilting your instruction a few degrees. Even positioning your voice to hit a side wall instead of the back wall can help with acoustics.
- **Breathe Fresh Air**- If you can't open your windows, take students to some fresh air from time to time. Get them to the outside of the building even for a few moments of fresh air.

ADDITIONAL DESIGN LENSES

How can we stay focused on what matters?

Effective design teams are always designing and considering new opportunities. Here are some additional questions in four essential areas that we can ask to keep the focus on what is best for kids.

1. **Trauma-Informed Spaces**

   How can this space heal? Where are the stressful places? Will these decisions support our students with their mental health needs? Do our spaces have a natural sense of safety? Will our spaces cause triggers or unneeded negative emotions?

2. **Profile of a Graduate**

   Do our spaces help our students grow as collaborators? Can our spaces make our students more successful after they leave our building? What about our spaces elevate our graduates' chances of happiness and prosperity in their pursuits? Will our space allow our students to contribute to the community now and in the future?

3. **Learning Differences**

   Are we designing spaces that support different rates of learning? Where are our spaces for students with advanced readiness? Do our spaces honor different paths and paces? Do we have spaces that negatively impact specific learning disabilities?

4. **Accessibility**

   Are we creating spaces that limit mobility? How can we make sure that materials and equipment are available for all to use? Is the density of our design inhibiting accessibility? How can those students with visual impairments best use our spaces?

FUNDING SPACES

Though some of the ideas in this book are free and available, transforming space is rarely a free exercise. We hope that this book has shown the benefits of redesign. Making learning spaces a budget priority can be difficult, but we believe that it is essential to supporting the future of learning. Here are some initial thoughts on some questions that we get asked about funding.

How do we convince people that we need funding?

- Our environment is essential for optimal well-being, and affects how we learn, collaborate and create meaning. It is the setting in which we cultivate our culture and community.

How do schools go about getting the funding for this work?

- Fundraising, capital campaigns, community donations, grants and gifts are all a part of the mix for most schools, but it is important to work for more dollars in the regular budgeting process.

Why should we spend money on learning spaces?

- The design of space can be a catalyst for the modernization of many systems in the school including curriculum design, instructional practices, and the infusion of technology.

How should we spend our money?

- Make a visible impact in one or two locations to start. Sprinkling a little change everywhere can diffuse the change to the point of it not being noticeable.

Where can we get the most value?

- Focus on spaces where learning happens the most. Big projects in spaces where learning rarely happens can be important, but are less likely to affect teaching and learning.

Think in Phases

Phase One: Learning

Phase one breaks the momentum. Redesigning learning spaces will help convince the teachers, students and the community of the importance of this work.

Phase Two: Culture, Community

Transform the spaces that affect your culture: entrances, welcome spaces, and more to reflect your mission and values.

Phase Three: Continued Growth

In this phase the teachers, students, and community push forward their own initiatives built around a common vision.

Legacy of the Space

Your school is a living and breathing learning space. It sees and hears. Are you in sync with your space? How is your vision alive in your learning spaces?

IS YOUR SPACE AN HONORABLE ASSET TO THE COMMUNITY?

WILL YOUR SPACE SUSTAIN FOR GENERATIONS OF LEARNERS AFTER YOU? DOES IT HONOR THOSE WHO HAVE PASSED THROUGH THE DOORS BEFORE YOU?

WHAT WILL THE LEGACY OF THE BUILDING BE?

THE LIVING BUILDING

DOES IT BREATHE LIFE INTO THE TEACHERS AND STUDENTS THAT IT SURROUNDS EACH DAY?

IS IT FILLED WITH WORDS THAT INSPIRE AND MOTIVATE?

IS YOUR BUILDING ENVIRONMENTALLY FRIENDLY?

Our learning spaces can be places where we go to complete our work and learning, or they can be a member of the ecosystem, supporting our health and well-being.

You get to choose.

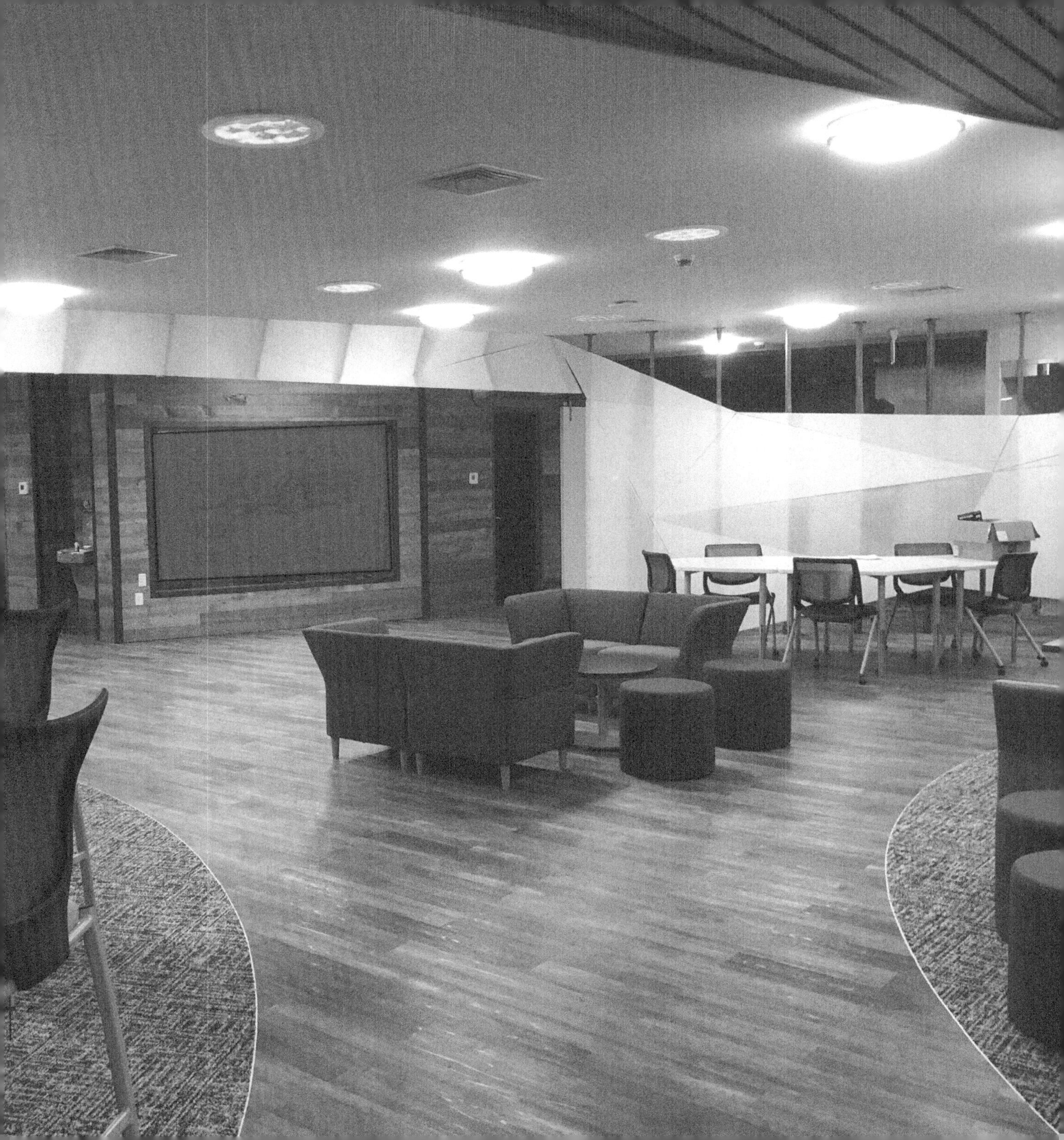

Do your students know your intention?

Dear Student,

This is what I want for you.

The learners of tomorrow that are truly not only college- and career-ready, but life-ready need to be learning in spaces that allow more collaboration, curiosity, and creativity to flourish. Imagine the typical classroom: it was never designed for the level of sophistication in learning that is happening in so many schools today.

Let's change this together by walking through our spaces and rethinking the physical, emotional, and digital spaces that surround our learning community. What do you need and want from your school? What are the possibilities?
We realize that there are budgets and legacy practices that are barriers, but we can come together and create amazing solutions and spaces for learning . The time has come to make this a priority.

By changing how and where we learn, we can better prepare you for a world of change that demands big thinkers who care deeply.

Signed,
Your Lead Learner

There are...

12,960

hours kids spend in school until they graduate.

Should they have the spaces in which they can thrive?

Will they remember their spaces as caring and supportive?

Is your community ready for better schools?

Do you need to begin this journey now?

YES

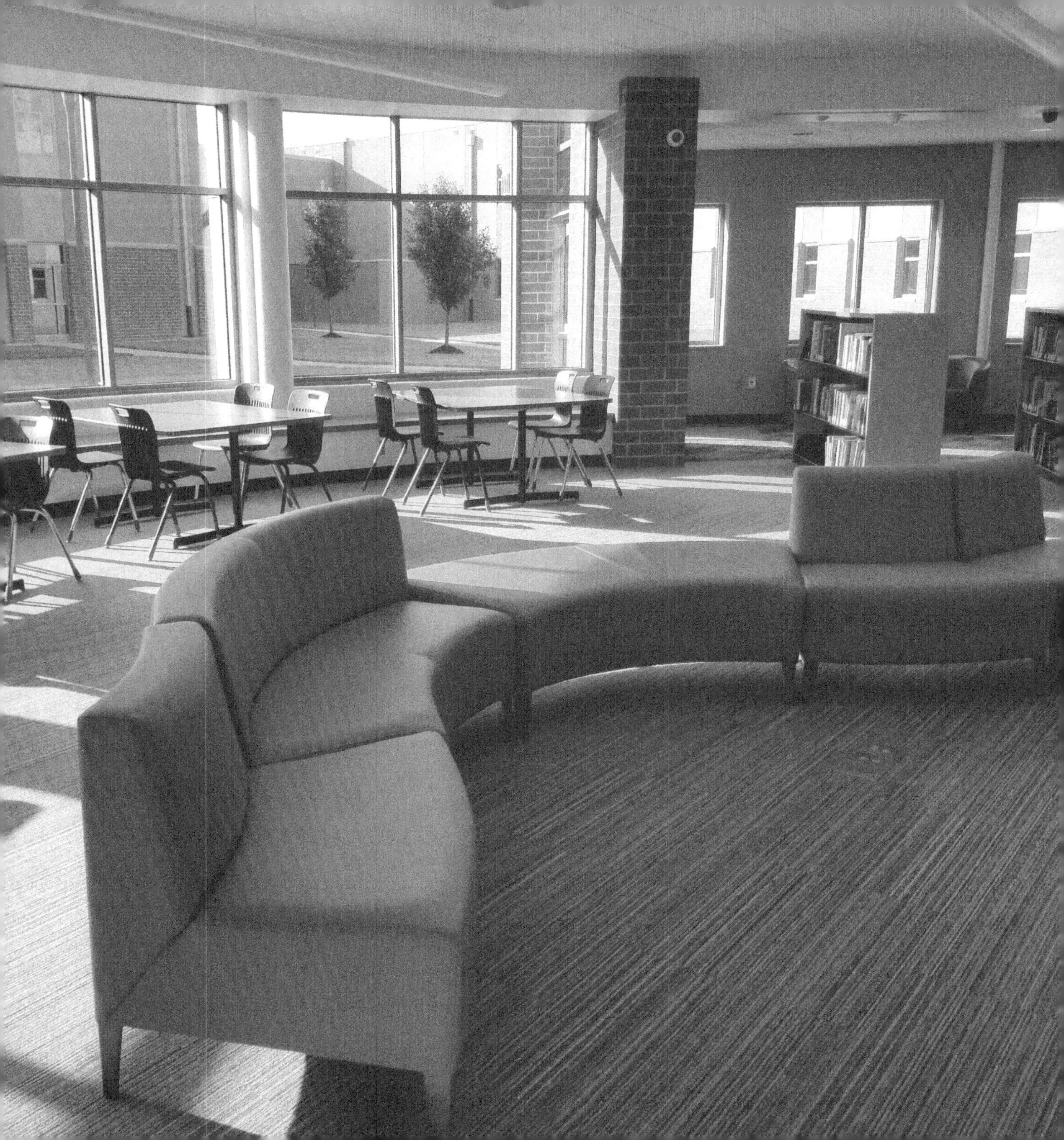

Final Reality Check...

THE SAYING, DOING GAP

We are student centered . . . but kids must sit in their desk to learn

We are data informed . . . but all we can discuss is one test

We care for children . . . but bells dictate our every move

We are focused on learning . . . but in a way that worked for us

We value community . . . but no one truly feels welcomed

We have a growth mindset . . but so much continues to be fixed

Resources/Research Mentioned

Barrett, P. et al. "The impact of classroom design on pupils' learning: Final results of a holistic, multi-level analysis." Building and Environment 89 (2015): 118-133.

Bayat, Nihat. "The Effect of the Process Writing Approach on Writing Success and Anxiety." *Educational Sciences: Theory & Practice*, 2014, doi:10.12738/estp.2014.3.1720.

Cowie, Bronwen, et al. *Expanding Notions of Assessment for Learning: inside Science and Technology Primary Classrooms*. SensePublishers, 2013.

Edelstein, E. and E. Macagno. "Form Follows Function: Bridging Neuroscience and Architecture." (2012).

Gertzman, Alice D. and J. Kolodner. "A case study of problem-based learning in a middle school science classroom: lessons learned." (1996).

Hammond, Zaretta, and Yvette Jackson. *Culturally Responsive Teaching and the Brain: Promoting Authentic Engagement and Rigor among Culturally and Linguistically Diverse Students*. Corwin, a SAGE Company, 2015.

Holmes, T. "The neuroscience of classrooms." Spaceoasis. Retrieved from www.spaceoasis.com/wp-content/uploads/2017/01/The-neuroscience-ofclassrooms-V1-Jan-2017.pdf (2017).

Hubenthal, M. and T. O'Brien. "Revisiting your classrooms' walls: The pedagogical power of posters." Retrieved from http://www.iris.edu/hq/files/programs/education_and_outreach/poster_pilot/Poster_Guide_v2a.pdf (2009).

Immordino-Yang, Mary Helen. *Emotions, Learning, and the Brain: Exploring the Educational Implications of Affective Neuroscience*. W.W. Norton & Company, 2016.

Katz, L. and S. C. Chard. "The Contribution of Documentation to the Quality of Early Childhood Education. ERIC Digest." (1996).

Leyba, Erin. "5 Guidelines for Giving Kids Choices." *Psychology Today*, Sussex Publishers, 1 Feb. 2016, www.psychologytoday.com/us/blog/joyful-parenting/201602/5-guidelines-giving-kids-choices.

Michal MaimaranClinical Associate Professor of Marketing; Research Associate Professor of Marketing. "Are You Offering Your Children Too Many Choices?" *Kellogg Insight*, insight.kellogg.northwestern.edu/article/choice-set-size-and-children.

Mitra, D. "The Significance of Students: Can Increasing Student Voice in Schools Lead to Gains in Youth Development?." Teachers College Record 106 (2004): 651-688.

Parrish, Nina. "How to Teach Self-Regulation." *Edutopia*, George Lucas Educational Foundation, 22 Aug. 2018, www.edutopia.org/article/how-teach-self-regulation.

Priestley, Mark, et al. *Teacher Agency: an Ecological Approach*. Bloomsbury Academic, 2019.

Reeve, J. and Ching-Mei Tseng. "Agency as a fourth aspect of students' engagement during learning activities." Fuel and Energy Abstracts (2011): n. Pag.

Sheets Rosa Hernandez., and Etta R. Hollins. *Racial and Ethnic Identity in School Practices: Aspects of Human Development*. L. Erlbaum Associates, 1999.

"Visible Thinking (Article)." *Visible Thinking (Article) | Project Zero*, www.pz.harvard.edu/resources/visible-thinking-article.

ABOUT THE AUTHORS

Rebecca Louise Hare is an author, speaker, educator, and a learning space designer. Rebecca has a BFA in industrial design from The European Design Institute in Milan, Italy and a M.A.T. in art from Fontbonne University, St. Louis. She worked in Italy for ten years as a design consultant and creative director, creating spaces and designing products (from MRI machines and coffee makers to hair brushes) for global companies before becoming fascinated with education. She found that the young designers she was hiring were struggling with solving problems and thinking critically. This brought her back to the United States to study education. Her master's thesis focused on design thinking, evaluating, and enhancing creativity through the study of design and art. She has taught art and design to pre-k-12 learners, fourth grade science, engineering and design.She collaborates and consults with schools designing learning spaces that enhance student learning. Rebecca is an Apple Distinguished Educator, Adobe Education Leader and Consultant and when she isn't in the classroom she is busy facilitating the design of learning environments and experiences that support creativity, design, design thinking and student agency.She's the mom of two curious learners and lives with her family in St. Louis.

Dr. Robert Dillon is Dr. Robert Dillon is an author, speaker, educator, and lifelong learner. His twenty plus years in education has seen him serve kids and families as a teacher, principal, technology director, and innovation leader. His primary focus is working to bring synergy to instructional design, technology infusion, and learning space design. He believes that in this synergy is the educational gold that students need to be successful citizens in a modern world. He works through an equity lens and looks to bring excellence to every classroom. For this work, he has been honored by Common Sense Media, The Center for Green Schools, the dSchool at Stanford University, the Buck Institute for Education, and Future Ready Schools. Dr. Dillon has had the opportunity to work with teachers and leaders throughout the country, and he continues to speak at local, regional, and national conferences. Dr. Dillon is the co-founder of ConnectED Learning, a Saint Louis non-profit dedicated to affordable, quality professional learning for teachers. He is the author of five books. He is supported in his work by his wife and two amazing daughters.

Made in the USA
Middletown, DE
17 April 2021